Blithe Tomato

Blithe Tomato

Mike Madison

Drawings by Patrick McFarlin

Foreword by Deborah Madison

Great Valley Books

Heyday Books, Berkeley, California

Names and circumstances have been changed for the usual reasons.

Library of Congress Cataloging-in-Publication Data
Madison, Mike, 1947-
  Blithe tomato / Mike Madison ; drawings by Patrick McFarlin.
    p. cm.
  ISBN 1-59714-024-4 (pbk. : alk. paper)
  1. Farm life—California—Anecdotes. 2. Farmers—California—Anecdotes. 3. Family farms—California—Anecdotes. 4. Madison, Mike, 1947- I. Title.
  S521.5.C2M33 2006
  917.94--dc22

                              2005029276

Cover Art: Patrick McFarlin
Book Design: Rebecca LeGates
Printing and Binding: McNaughton and Gunn, Saline, MI

Orders, inquiries, and correspondence should be addressed to:
    Heyday Books
    P. O. Box 9145, Berkeley, CA 94709
    (510) 549-3564, Fax (510) 549-1889
    www.heydaybooks.com

Printed in the United States of America

10 9 8 7 6 5 4 3 2 1

Contents

April 2

July 11

October 7

Foreword

Deborah Madison

SAN FRANCISCO IN THE MID-1970S was starting to be a heady and exciting place to cook, with all the new foods that were appearing on the scene. Arugula, goat cheese, and sun-dried tomatoes were making their debuts on restaurant tables. Farmer friends who were willing to give it a go were planting, in addition to the arugula, Marvel of Four Seasons lettuce and dozens of other varieties, exotic fingerling potatoes, skinny green beans, fava beans, and shell beans, and the first heirloom tomatoes. And a few ranchers were starting to produce amazing lamb and pork, and zinfandel was coming off the vineyards. Herbs were bountiful. Bushy bouquets of borage, chives, scented basils, and lovage filled a shelf on my walk-in at Greens. The notion that there was virtue to be found in "locally grown, seasonal foods"— now a phrase as flat and overused as "fresh"—was gathering strength, although we weren't using those words. Naturally, these foods were local and in season, because they were being grown just up the road, over the bridge, and in some cases, down the block; and food that's cooked where it's grown is, of course, in season.

The handful of chefs and farmers I knew who were in search of a symbiotic working relationship were optimistic that small, specialized farms would grow in number, along with like-minded cooks. But none of us could possibly have looked into the future and see that, twenty-five years later, there would be gorgeous produce all over the country, impressive American farmstead cheeses and well-raised, good-tasting meats, and that any chef worth her hand-harvested sea salt would be cooking with foods that were organically and sustainably raised, preferably right down the road. We failed to imagine that there would be four thousand farmers' markets around the nation, or that a book like *Blithe Tomato* would ever be written. It was way too early for *Blithe Tomato*.

In 1990, well after the start of this whole movement, I moved to a new city and volunteered to manage the local farmers' market, and that's when I began to see how much work it would take for this benign activity—making good foods available to shoppers and chefs—to continue. The merits of the market were obvious: the incomparable taste, the bloom of freshness, the new varieties of plants and animals, the old ones brought back. It was fun running into friends and planning impromptu dinners, and it was rewarding to connect with those who grow our food, to get to know them and their farms. I could also see that small-scale organic farming was good for the landscape, for wildlife habitat, for those rural communities so often left behind economically, even for our mental and physical health. But I saw farmers becoming discouraged, quitting and going back to work for regular pay, or simply growing old and selling their farms to people looking for country homes. Didn't we need to garner support and understanding for the hard work and low pay endured by farmers? Didn't we need to encourage new ones?

Like *Blithe Tomato*, my own homage to farmers is a book, *Local Flavors: Cooking and Eating from Farmers' Markets*. I wanted people to understand something about the difficulty of farming, so that price might cease to be the basis for choosing what to eat. I wanted to focus on the implications that our food choices have, not only for the pleasures of the table, but for the quality of life that revolves around good, small-scale food production. Then there was the notion that "in season" is where we live, not some vague generalized concept, and the promise of astonishment that would come from encounters with the immediacy of real food.

This endeavor was enormously appealing, as many other writers have found, because here's a situation that firmly drives a wedge into the business-as-usual system of agriculture. Becoming a farmers' market shopper is not only smart and fun, but a politically powerful act that has the ability to effect change in communities all around the country. And with millions of consumers taking their dollars to the farmers' market, farmers have at last begun to emerge from their fields. They get photographed and interviewed on a fairly regular basis. They have websites, they are invited to Slow Food dinners, they are featured in *Gourmet,* and they are now, in short, the sung heroes of many. This is good.

But what we haven't heard much of, yet, is the farmer's voice, and this brings us back to Mike Madison's *Blithe Tomato,* a book that really conveys the gritty, complex substance of the farming life. Frankly, I find it a relief to hear from a farmer—rather than a farmer-sympathizer like me—about what it means to do what he does. After all, it's the farmer who knows the big picture, the one that includes, along with the misery of drought and dust, the begrudged sharing of crops with creatures, and the irritating assumptions made by customers, the pleasures that farm life brings—a surprise visit with a mouse and her family, a cascade of bird song interrupting the morning, the satisfaction of being one's own boss, even when the pay is far from plentiful.

Mike Madison mainly grows flowers, thousands of them, food for the soul. And he's spent enough years behind his table at the farmers' market, talking with customers, chatting with fellow farmers, and closely observing the world he inhabits, to have formed a wealth of opinions about people and food. Telling it like it is in a piece on weeding, he chides people like me who gasp at neatly laid out rows of newly weeded lettuce and immediately, with perhaps a dash of envy, imbue the work of farming with symmetry and calm. Hours spent planting thousands of bulbs give him time to raise some interesting questions, such as "Is slovenliness an infectious disease?" He admits to the bad days and dreams of escape. He cites poems and prose and prints to-do lists that will humble all but the most industrious among us. There are family stories, gossip about the market shoppers, and musings on such subjects as dogs, tomatoes, mowing, foraging, birds and raccoons, the virtues of local economies, beautiful women, and gophers. The chapter on gophers, I'm convinced, will stop all but the most blindly stubborn would-be farmer from ever planting a thing.

For readers who wish to have a deeper connection with those who grow our food, it's a bonus that Mike paints not only his own picture, but shares the lives of his fellow farmers with affection and sympathy, creating in the end a group portrait of people who have come to do what they do for all kinds of reasons. Failing or succeeding in different degrees, farmers are human beings who are moved by their obsessions, their follies, their industry or lack of it. Like any of us. But they're also moved by that strange and compelling lust to plant a seed and see what will come of it, and they have a certain toughness that makes them willing to live on the edge of our consumption-driven culture, where they can plant those seeds again and again, gophers or not.

As we learn in these stories, the farming life is indeed rife with frustration, but *Blithe Tomato* is no plea for sympathy. This farmer holds his own, even if there are days when moving to one of the Lesser Falkland Islands has its appeal. Still, I've no doubt that the reader will come to the last page of *Blithe Tomato* and then close the cover with great respect for the determination of the small farmer. Some of us might even feel a need to scratch around and see if we can't come up with some such measure of true grit in our own lives. I, for one, am grateful to my brother Mike for being able to work two jobs (farming and writing) at once, for *Blithe Tomato* is a deeply touching account of the farming life. These wry, sometimes aching, and always delightful stories will be inhaled by the reader as hungrily as one drinks in the fragrance of lilacs or the perfume of a Venus grape. And as the food we cook can't be any better than the ingredients we start with, no matter how brilliantly we shape them, we all owe a huge debt of thanks to these farmers who bring good food so close to home.

Deborah Madison (Mike's sister) was the founding chef of Greens restaurant in San Francisco and is the author of Local Flavors: Cooking and Eating from America's Farmers' Markets *and other books.*

Blithe Tomato

January 4

Repair leaking skylight, toolshed
Order 25 tons compost for citrus
Pick up 5 crates lily bulbs
Plant lily bulbs
Set gopher traps — olive trees row 11, row 14
Finish pruning apricots
Order melon seeds
Order sunflower seeds
Weed ranunculus beds
Weed tulip beds
Bottle 4 cases olive oil for market
Pick 6 boxes of clementines for the co-op
Clementines and oranges to the food bank
Income tax
File organic registration
Prune quince trees
Stick lavender cuttings — 4 flats
Pick up oil, gear oil, hydraulic fluid, grease, filters
Service tractor, bed shaper
Replace shear pin, flail mower
Order gravel for road
Cut and split fallen walnut tree for firewood
Review budget for farmers' market
    directors meeting
Change oil in Chevy
Transplant late crop of kale
Stake sweet peas

Cultivation

I'VE NOTICED AN ODD THING. The commonest weed in my lettuce beds is lettuce—not lettuce, the crop, but wild lettuce, *Lactuca seriola*. It looks enough like the other lettuces, but it is too prickly and bitter to eat. Even the slugs leave it alone. So I find myself hoeing in the lettuce beds, muttering, "Damned lettuce." A farmer's joke.

It's not just lettuce. Endives, which I quit growing ten years ago, and unwisely let go to seed, are still coming up. There are wild carrots lurking about the carrot beds; nightshade slipping into a bed with its cousin, the potato; and wild barley, in these parts called foxtails, infesting the barley field. It seems that almost every crop has some unsavory relation hanging about the place.

There are sound agronomic reasons for this. The kinds of plants best suited to domestication are those that thrive in an open and disturbed habitat, like a farm; that grow rapidly and splendidly; and that make seeds in abundance. These also are traits of weeds. So crops and weeds are shadows of one another, and it is an irony of farming that the farmer must work so hard at this shadow play.

It is not just the vegetable beds that need cultivating. The farmer must also cultivate himself, for he too has his weedy tendencies. He has to be vigilant at chopping out those coarse and hairy thoughts that threaten to overwhelm more tender notions, and at uprooting bitter and prickly attitudes that make him unfit for the table. Like weeding the beds, this is a task that will never be finished.

A passerby, chancing along on an auspicious day, might look at my lettuce beds and think, "How effortlessly the lettuces grow, springing from the earth in neat rows. And what an idyllic and uncomplicated life the farmer leads, plucking up these lovely crops and taking them to market." But the passerby does not see, in a dark corner of the barn, the heap of hoes, their steel nearly worn away with the labor of cultivating. Nor does he sense, behind the farmer's congenial smile, a certain shadow.

Lonesome Youth

A LONESOME YOUTH WALKS to and fro in the market. He's dressed all in black: black trousers about fifteen sizes too big, black t-shirt, black leather bands around his wrists. His hair is dyed black and tortured into spikes. I think maybe he has black eye shadow. He has half a dozen earrings in each ear, and metal studs in his lip and his cheeks and his eyebrows and the side of his nose, and probably in other places I'd just as soon not know about.

He walks back and forth through the market, a look of agony on his face. He seems not to notice the heaps of produce on either side, and he never buys anything. The farmers look at one another and wink, or roll their eyes, secretly giving thanks that their own sons have not slid so far. But I regard him with sympathy. For I was once that way myself. Not that I dressed that way—I didn't. When I was fifteen years old I attended boarding school in New England, and we wore coats and ties, and had unremarkable haircuts. The similarity between my former self and the youth in black is in the condition of our souls. At that age I radiated waves of existential anguish powerful enough to topple a porcelain vase at a distance of twenty feet.

Clothing is a statement of fashion, and at one level the youth in black is merely conforming to the fashion of his peers. But clothing is also symbolic. That his trousers are fifteen sizes too big I take as his expression of feeling insufficient to fill the oversized expectations that society has of him. And all those lumps of metal in his flesh— what can they be but symbolic bullets? For who living among us, and paying any attention at all, does not feel assaulted?

Ali

ONE EVENING MY WIFE AND I WERE TALKING about vacations, and the question came up of when the last time was that we took a week off and went somewhere. It turned out it was 1983, more than twenty years ago. In the year just past, which had been an especially bad one, bracketed by large failures and punctuated by small failures, I had worked 362 days out of 365, dawn to dark, for a net farm income of $19,730.

Most of the small farmers are caught in the same trap. The little farms are so unprofitable that the farmer can't afford to hire help, and so he ends up doing the work of three men. Some become discouraged, some become injured, and many drop out, but there are a few of us stubborn old goats who hang in there year after year.

I am not the hardest working farmer at the market, however. That would be Ali. Ali is a Pakistani immigrant who grows fruit—apples and pears, cherries and plums, nectarines, peaches, apricots, persimmons, and a dozen varieties of citrus. He runs his orchards by himself and puts in the same kind of hours I do, with one added burden. Five nights a week, from eleven at night until seven the next morning, he drives a forklift in a warehouse.

Ali bought his land in April, and though it was really too late, he was determined to plant his trees the same year. He sat down with a huge pile of catalogues and began calling nurseries all over the West, buying whatever bare-root trees they still had in cold storage. Ali had a theory about buying fruit trees, and his theory—not a bad one—

was "ten of everything." And so he had 280 peach trees: ten each of twenty-eight varieties. If he had planted all one variety, he would have peaches for eight or ten days; with twenty-eight varieties, he had peaches for fifteen weeks. The other fruits—apples and cherries and the rest—were equally diverse: ten of this, ten of that, ten of another. Because of the very late planting time, Ali planted out the trees as soon as they arrived from the nurseries, without any particular order to them, so that the various sorts were randomly mixed on his land. This was not a rational arrangement, and it confounded irrigation and spraying and harvesting and every other aspect of orchard management. On the other hand, it confused his enemies, too. A little block of ten pear trees might get fire blight, but the next group of ten pear trees was five rows away and might well go unscathed. If the pears had all been in one block, the disease would affect all of them.

One Wednesday night I noticed Ali walking through the market on his way to get a tamale. Everything about him spelled fatigue—the tilt of his head, the droop of his mustache, the sagging dark semicircles under his eyes. He walked with the fatalistic and dejected gait of one who knowingly persists in a futile enterprise, unable to find a way out. He greeted me cheerfully, though (imagine a heavy Pakistani accent):

"Hey, Mike, how's it going?"

"Okay," I said. "The gophers are leaving me a little something to sell. I'm kind of tired, though." Ali sighed and nodded in commiseration. "I suppose we can rest when we're dead," I said.

To my surprise, Ali vigorously shook his head "no" at this platitude and, raising a finger in a stern gesture, he said, "I don't think so, Mike. I worry about Judgment Day, you know. God will say to me, 'I gave you life, and what did you do with it? You wasted the whole thing working.' He is a tough judge, you know. He will not be happy with us."

Ali is a devoted follower of Islam, and while I admire his fidelity, his religion is as incomprehensible to me as Christianity. I think you have to be born into those religions. I grew up in a skeptical and irreligious household, and the kind of church I might belong to at this stage, the Reformed Druidic Animists, isn't to be found in my area. And so I belong to no church, though I am not irreverent.

As to whether God would chastise me for overwork, I do not know. For myself, I make no distinction between work and play. If I were to win sixty million dollars in the lottery, I might replace the broken radio in my '86 Chevy, but beyond that I don't think that I would do anything different from what I'm already doing. So I could make the case that I do no work at all, I'm simply playing.

Judgment Day. I imagine myself in the vestibule of heaven, waiting in a line defined by frayed velvet ropes hanging from chromium bollards. Finally, my turn comes. I step up to the keyboard and follow the instructions on the screen, using the tab key to move from box to box, filling in the information. When I'm done I hit the Enter key. I hear the whirring sound of an old dot-matrix printer (did they buy this rig from Ross Perot in the seventies?) and my judgment card is extruded from a little slot.

At the top of my judgment card is my name, and my parents names, and my place and date of birth, and place and date of death. Box number nine is labeled "Judgment Score, Scale of 100." Good lord! It's a 63! Why, that's a low D, barely a passing grade. I thought I had led a better life than that. I was a hard worker, reasonably honest, frequently sober. Where had I slipped up? Was I a negligent son and an oblivious father? Had I made too many impious jokes? Had I been too lax at stomping on those lascivious mental cockroaches that scuttle around in my brain? Wait, what's this? Box ten, Principal Personal Defect. An 'H' is printed in the box. I turn the card over. On the back, in pale blue type, is an explanation of the personal defect code. Here it is, "H": "Insufficient Joy."

Insufficient joy. Make a joyful noise unto the lord, all ye lands. And I was silent. So Ali was right, after all. But what else could we have done, given our circumstances?

Gophers

THE REASON WHY I AM SOMETIMES TEMPTED to quit farming in disgust, and the reason why I can never quit farming, are the same. The reason is a little burrowing rodent called the western pocket gopher. The word "pocket" in his name refers to a pouch on each side of his face in which he can carry his lunch. I have trapped gophers with their pockets stuffed with grains of wheat and oats, or chunks of radish, or half a tulip bulb.

The gopher is a vegetarian, and lives by eating the farmer's crops. He prefers the most expensive ones, and will always choose Casablanca lilies over mere tulips. He lives underground in a maze of tunnels. There is generally just one gopher to a system of tunnels, which makes me wonder how it is that they breed so prolifically. Perhaps on Saturday nights Mr. Gopher slicks back his hair with his little paw, and polishes his ugly yellow teeth on a bit of root, and dabs some fennel under his arms, and goes above ground looking for a date. He whistles one up, or follows her pheromones, or maybe just goes to a club. Having found each other, he and Ms. Gopher knock off a quick and anonymous coupling in the grass—a squirm and a squirt—before going their separate ways. Some humans don't do much better.

I reckon that I lose 25 percent of my net income to gophers. Each year I write that check: Pay to the order of Gopher, Six thousand and 00/100 dollars. That's the difference between retiring when I'm sixty-five and working until the day I drop dead in the field with a hoe in my hand. And so I keep after the gophers. I've made what I think is a generous deal with them. There's a six-acre block of forest along the creek where the gophers are free to build their civilizations however they choose, to develop the arts and sciences, to devote themselves to politics or literature, to pursue lives of asceticism or debauchery, and I will not interfere. But once they leave their own country and come into the cultivated lands, then they become fair targets, and I try to trap them.

Trapping consists of digging into the burrows, which are not always easily found, and setting a little wire trap, one facing each way, and then closing up the hole. When the unsuspecting gopher comes along and bumps into the trap, a powerful spring squeezes him around the thorax, and when he exhales he is unable to inhale again, and so he suffocates. I lie in bed trying to imagine this, and it is not pleasant. The wire trap is said to be humane, "humane" being an ironic term referring to the lesser of two atrocities. Sometimes the trap doesn't work correctly, and the gopher dies a horrible slow death. When this happens, I bury him at the base of a tree and say a little prayer: "May your bones nourish this tree, and may your spirit be reincarnated as a tree swallow so that you might experience the world wheeling in the open sky instead of lurking in a muddy tunnel."

In choosing enemies, one must be even more careful than in choosing friends. Too powerful an enemy will crush your spirit; too weak an enemy affords no scope for sport or honor. As enemies go, the gopher is a good choice. He is wily and not easily caught, and ten times out of eleven my trap is empty. And the gopher is easy to hate because he is a vandal. Look here, at this young olive tree, with a trunk as thick as a broom handle, a fine little tree, growing lustily in every direction. One day you notice that it looks a bit water stressed. You reach down to feel the ground, your finger breaks through into an underground cavity, and the tree falls over sideways, bitten off where the root joins the stem. The gopher kills an eighty-pound tree to take a quarter ounce of food, and instead of staying there to finish the meal, he goes on to the next tree, and kills it too. If one weren't a congenital pessimist, it would be heartbreaking. And yet, there is something cowardly about trapping. I never meet my enemy face to face. I put the trap in a burrow, and the next morning

I pull out a little corpse on the end of a wire. If I had to kill him face to face, say, by decapitating him with a sharp spade, and if I had to look into his bright, terrified eyes, I don't know that I could do it. In trapping, the relationship is I-it; but face to face it becomes I-thou, and it would do violence to my notion of myself to slaughter the little fellow so unceremoniously.

I don't know how a Hindu or a Buddhist would deal with this, but I can tell you that he would not be in the olive tree business. One winter I planted a little grove of twelve hundred olive trees into clean, gopher-free ground. But gophers snuck in that spring under cover of some clover, and the first summer I trapped 191 gophers out of the grove, and they killed just under three hundred trees. If I had not trapped them, they would have killed all of the trees, just as one winter when I wasn't paying attention they ate every single bulb out of a bed of two thousand tulips.

I set twenty-six traps each day, which takes an hour of my time. Trapping is a job about which I can never say, "There! That's it. I'm done." It's like bailing out a rapidly leaking boat—a condition of existence. I feed the dead gophers to some half-feral cats that hang about the place. In theory, the cats are supposed to catch the gophers, but they are smarter than I am and have figured out that if they just lie about on the porch, I will bring gophers to them. I have wondered if there is a higher use for the carcasses. I have thought of applying taxidermy to them and creating kitsch dioramas—gophers playing poker, Washington crossing the Delaware, Munch's "The Scream"—that sort of thing. But I haven't done it.

On a particularly bad day, one is tempted to shake a fist at the heavens and cry out, "Why, God, did you make this odious creature?" And having asked the question, one readily thinks of an answer. For, among animals who are vandals, the first prize certainly goes to humans, the most destructive of all creatures; none of the others come even close. And so the gopher is there to play the role played by the buffoon and the zany in a comic opera. He is there to mock us by clumsily imitating us, and to remind us of our own environmental crimes. This is almost fair. But there is a deep injustice in the way it's carried out, for those least culpable are most afflicted. In Washington, D.C., where they are badly needed, there are no gophers at all.

Byron Shedd

The market was coming to an end, we had sold out, and we were sitting on the tailgate of a pickup, talking with our friend Dave. "That Byron Shedd, he's quite a ladies' man," said Dave.

My wife, bless her, burst out laughing. "That little twerp? A ladies' man?" she laughed again.

"He told me so himself," said Dave defensively.

"Egotism thrives in the most unlikely places," I observed. As for Byron being a ladies' man, it might be true. There are some women so empathetic and accommodating that they will play whatever role is expected of them out of sheer agreeableness, and because of them, thinking of oneself as a ladies' man can become a self-fulfilling prophecy.

Now past fifty, Byron Shedd had a substantial potbelly, and rapidly thinning sandy hair, and the kind of light, freckled skin that ages badly in a hot climate. He was probably of average height, but he gave the impression of being short, perhaps because of the way he walked with his nose in the air.

Byron had been a pioneer organic farmer in the back-to-the-land movement of the 1970s. He and his wife, Lisa Chang, had leased ten acres of good land north of town and starting farming it. The farm prospered, and they bought the land they had leased and neighboring blocks as well. It was Lisa who was the farmer of the two. She had a knack for farming, and the crews of Mexican workers, at first uneasy about working for a woman, became devoted to her. Byron loved being a farmer, but didn't much care for the actual farming part of it. He was a farmer in the same way that Ronald Reagan was president. In his few meager attempts at the day-to-day labor of farming, Byron found it to be hard, tiresome, and boring work, and he was happy to leave the running of the farm to Lisa. Ten o'clock in the morning would find him sitting at the kitchen table with his friend Jim, starting in on the third pot of coffee, and talking about the theory of agriculture.

There was not an alternative farming conference, or organic seminar, or populist gathering, that Byron did not attend. He had some old blue jeans with patches on the knees, faded flannel shirts, and a weatherbeaten hat that he wore on these occasions. He would take the stand and speak out in ringing tones about the plight of small farmers like himself, surviving by pure courage and grit in the face of competition from evil agribusiness, battered but undaunted. He brought a stirring message from the true tiller of the soil, and during dramatic pauses in his oratory he would look around the audience and make eye contact with any attractive woman he hoped he might get together with afterward. These were inspiring talks, but when you shook hands with him you knew right away that he was a fraud; his hands were as soft as a baby's cheek.

After twenty-two years of marriage, Byron and Lisa divorced. She was tired of his pompous ranting, and his utter uselessness around the farm, and his undependability, and his philandering. Byron was legally an equal partner in the land and in the farming enterprise, and he walked off with a sizeable cash settlement. He used some of it to buy a ruined villa in Tuscany, more appealing in the idea than the reality. He liked to bring up his villa in conversation; he thought it gave him a cosmopolitan air, which you could almost believe until you heard him try to speak Italian.

Another term of the divorce granted Byron the right to take produce from Lisa's farm and sell it at the farmers' market. He would drive out to the farm on a Friday night and back his van up to the walk-in coolers, where he would pick through their produce, selecting whatever he thought might sell. A hired assistant picked up the van at five thirty in the morning and drove it to market and set up the display. Byron would show up about ten and stand around the produce, striking farmerly poses for fifteen or twenty minutes until someone showed up he could go out to coffee with. He came back about twelve-thirty to count the money. The other farmers in the market regarded Byron with a mixture of amusement and contempt, and when he paraded through the market, his progress was followed by muttered oaths and rude jokes.

One day I happened to pick up the published proceedings of a farm conference. I flipped it open and starting reading in the middle of a piece about small farms. The author described the long hours of back-breaking labor, the social isolation, and the discouragement of crop failures and fickle markets in what seemed to be an authentic voice. It was cogent and well-argued. I turned back to see who the author was, and was surprised to see that it was Byron Shedd, who I knew hadn't done an honest day's work in twenty years. I looked at the article in my hand—a manifest Kierkegaardian paradox: true words, spoken by a false man.

Dogs

OF THE FOURTEEN HOUSEHOLDS IN MY NEIGHBORHOOD, twelve keep dogs. One of the landowners raises sheep, and his dogs are working dogs. The sheep dogs are well trained, and it is a pleasure to watch them practice their profession, which they do with skill and enthusiasm. On the other eleven places, the dogs are kept for pleasure, or perhaps for penance: it's not clear which.

One of my neighbors has three dogs, and he allows them to run loose. They are happy animals. They live as dogs are meant to live, trotting around, smelling the good smells, and chasing jackrabbits or the UPS truck. They remind me of a band of ten-year-old boys on their bicycles on a Saturday morning, roaming about and exploring, without destination or purpose. These dogs have no sense of land ownership, and they regularly wander through my place, doing nearly as much damage as gophers. They'll chase a jackrabbit down a bed of tulips and across the peonies, snapped-off buds flying in every direction. I have dropped less-than-subtle hints to the owner, but he doesn't get it. He says, "Oh yeah, you should have seen those dogs chasing a rabbit through a field of bell peppers. There were peppers flying everywhere. It was hilarious."

A couple of the neighborhood dogs are kept inside, and coddled, and fed scraps of prime rib and salmon fillets from the table. Their owners talk the most appalling baby talk to them without giving a guest sufficient warning so that he can quickly depart, or at least take some Dramamine. A couple of other dogs are well behaved and well cared for; they have been taught good manners, and they are let inside at night, and taken for a daily walk.

The rest of the dogs, amounting to half of them, are locked up in little cages, sometimes for months at a time. They are bored and lonely. They work in shifts, barking, all through the night and most of the day. Late at night a jackrabbit will hop past one of the pens, and that dog will start barking, and pretty soon the other dogs join in, and it takes an hour and a half for them to settle down. Then the rabbit passes by again, headed in the opposite direction, and the performance is repeated. The dogs' owners don't hear this; they're inside their houses, all the windows shut tight, the air conditioner humming, the TV blaring. One of my neighbors is a veterinarian. Apparently he believes that a cacophony of barking dogs is the natural sound of the universe, for he has never heard anything different. And so he keeps some endlessly barking mutts around his place in order to correct the unnerving quiet of the countryside.

About equal in number to the dogs in the neighborhood are their wild cousins, the coyotes. The coyotes are proud and independent creatures. They do not bark, though sometimes they sing. They are the only animals besides humans that sing in harmony, and it is a beautiful sound. One December when I was running behind schedule I spent a memorable evening planting tulips by moonlight while coyotes sang the bulbs into their beds. There are some ignorant and violent farmers in the region who shoot coyotes whenever they see them, giving as an excuse that coyotes are killers of sheep and poultry. Yet careful studies have shown that sheep kills and poultry kills attributed to coyotes are almost always the work of feral dogs. Coyotes live on rodents, and are the farmer's allies.

I have never been a dog owner myself, but I am not hostile to dogs. Over the years I have been friends with some very fine dogs. But for every excellent dog I've known, there have been three dozen others that were miserable. Dogs have thrown in their lot with humans, and dog society is a mirror of human society. Some are pampered, some are beaten, most are locked up and denied their freedom. A century ago none of these dogs would have been locked up. They would have spent the day in the company of their masters, gathering eggs, and plowing with a team of mules, and tending irrigation in an orchard. But the dignity of human labor has eroded, and the fortunes of dogs have declined correspondingly. The humans are confined in their cubicles, and the dogs in their pens. The modern human looks through a tiny window at a rectangle of sky and is troubled by a vague memory of freedom. He barks half-heartedly, wanly protesting his fate.

Beautiful Women

THE MARKET WHERE I SELL IS FAMOUS, among the farmers, for the beautiful women who shop there. It is a university town, and there are many students among the shoppers. Some are so graceful in motion, and so beautiful—with golden skin, and thick hair, and clear eyes—that one is tempted to kneel on the pavement and remove one's cap, as if in the presence of divinity. Many of the older women are also good-looking—fit and energetic and well-dressed. My friend James, who sells kiwi fruit, says, "I've never had a job quite like this. I just stand here and beautiful women come up to me and smile, and give me money."

I believe that what makes this crowd attractive is not so much the way they look as the unmistakable sparkle of intelligence. If a woman who looks like a movie star—physically perfect—opens her mouth and says something profoundly stupid, then her beauty immediately vanishes, or at least shrinks quite a bit. On the other hand, a woman of slightly odd, or even peculiar, appearance who says something witty and subversive is immediately attractive. (To be sure, beauty is in the eye of the beholder, and depends on how drunk the beholder is in whose eye this beauty is lodged, for there are states of inebriation in which inane conversation is no detriment—it can even be an asset.)

Former president Jimmy Carter, a deeply moral man, said that if he looked on a woman not his wife with amorous notions, he felt he had thereby committed an act of infidelity. His successor, Bill

Clinton, seemed to hold the identical philosophy, but carried it to its next logical step, which is that if the thought constitutes the sin, then there would be no further harm done by throwing in the physical act as well. I disagree with those two gentlemen. I believe that there is a great difference between exercising one's imagination and exercising one's zipper. And I find the former relatively harmless. I fall in love easily—at the drop of a hat even, or a skirt—but these little fantasies are ephemeral and of no consequence. It seems an odd remnant of Puritanism to be ashamed of belonging to a species whose members find one another attractive. Would it be better if we found one another repulsive?

Whether other species think this way, we do not know. Imagine the post-middle-aged bear down at the stream, having a drink. He looks up and sees, on the opposite bank, a lovely female bear standing on her hind limbs, gathering fruit. He thinks, "What magnificent fur, and look at the way she stands so gracefully, swaying slightly back and forth. How feminine." And then she turns her head and he thinks, "Oh my, look at that big wet nose. It will haunt my dreams."

At this point in the narrative, the Carter bear feels the clutch of remorse, and the Clinton bear splashes across the stream and ambles up the bank to introduce himself. But the old farmer bear just finishes his drink and takes a last look, and goes on his way thinking to himself, "What an excellent universe it is to be so amply provided with loveliness."

Dried Tomatoes

In the long hot summers of the late 1950s, I used to pick tomatoes for pocket money. Tomato fields covered the countryside, and every town had a cannery: Del Monte, Contadina, Libby's, Campbell's Soup. In our town it was Hunt's. I would kneel in the row, gathering ripe tomatoes into a pail, and when the pail was full I would carry it to the end of the row and empty it into a wooden lug box. The lug box held about fifty pounds, and I was paid sixteen cents a lug. Most of the other pickers were Mexican men. I enjoyed the strange sound of Spanish banter and snatches of song, and the distinctive smell of tomato foliage, which steadily stained my clothes and skin green. For each lug I filled, the foreman put a check mark by my name. At the end of the day I was paid in cash.

Arriving home on my bicycle I would flop onto my bed and study my money—a couple of dollars. The paper money didn't interest me much, but I liked the coins, especially the half dollar. On one side was the Walking Liberty, a sturdy and purposeful woman with flowing robes and flowing hair, striding across an agrarian landscape. She carries what appears to be an armload of rhubarb. Perhaps she intends to make a pie. Even to a child that symbolism was obvious enough, and I formed in my mind a Jeffersonian association of the notions of liberty, agriculture, and wealth.

After a break of some years, I'm back in the tomato fields again. This time the fields are my own. A February day finds me in the greenhouse sowing tomato seeds, while the tentacles of a winter storm lash at the eaves: one seed to a cell, ninety-six cells to a flat, sixteen flats to a bench. By March, the weather is warmer, and the little plants are up. Each day I stroke them with the palm of my hand, which makes the seedlings sturdier. By mid-April the ground is warm enough, and the tomato plants go outside.

We don't sell fresh tomatoes at the market—there are already too many other growers in that niche—so we just keep a few vines of Brandywine and Dona and Early Girl for our own use—salads, and open-face tomato sandwiches on toasted sourdough, or just for eating out of hand, like peaches. And my youngest daughter gets her plant of Sweet 100, for treats. Our commercial interest in tomatoes is for drying them. We grow a small Italian paste tomato, Principe Borghese, for this purpose. It makes little oval tomatoes, about the size and shape of a quail egg, in astronomical numbers. Harvest runs from July into September.

The tomatoes are small, but close enough together that you can grab half a dozen in each handful. I yank the vines out of the ground by the roots and take a load of them to the barn, where I can stand comfortably in the shade, plucking off the fruit and listening to Schubert on the radio. It doesn't take long to fill a lug, which these days is plastic rather than wood. I hose the dust off the fruit and set the boxes under an olive tree to drain. We slice the tomatoes lengthwise and set them face up on screens in the sun to dry. The tomato fruit has bilateral symmetry, like a person, and one soon comes to recognize the subtle bulge that lets one split it perfectly across the two chambers. No need for fancy German knives—a cheap little knife with a plastic handle and a serrated edge works great.

In our summer heat (100 degrees, no humidity) the tomatoes dry in a few days into crispy round wafers about the size of a nickel, in color dark red tending to black. Their texture shows their kinship to chiles. We store them in a freezer to keep pests out, and pack them in retail bags only when we're ready to take them to market the following winter. It takes about twenty-four pounds of fresh tomatoes to make one pound of dried.

To bring the dried tomatoes back to life, put a handful in a bowl, cover with boiling water, and let stand a minute or two. They can be used in soups and stews or salads, or spread on toast, but we use them almost exclusively with pasta: linguini with olive oil, garlic, and sun-dried tomatoes is often our winter meal three nights out of the week. The tomatoes have an extraordinary intensity of flavor, not much reminiscent of fresh tomatoes, but something unto itself.

We have a neighbor a dozen miles to the west who produces sun-dried tomatoes on a huge scale, reckoned in tons. He has apricot orchards as well, and when the season for drying apricots is finished he switches to tomatoes, using the same trays and drying yard. He grows canning tomatoes, which can be harvested mechanically; they are chopped by a machine and raked out onto the drying trays. This is very efficient, and his cost of production is half our cost. But the aesthetics of the result are poor—a sticky mass of dismembered tomato parts. In a soup this might be okay, but with pasta I find it worth the labor and expense to have those perfect little round wafers of dried Principe Borghese tomatoes, so that the eye is pleased as much as the palate.

Even if I weren't growing tomatoes for their fruit, I might still grow a few for the distinctive smell of their foliage. For me that odor is powerfully evocative of an early time. And it still sometimes brings to mind that childish interest in a half-dollar coin, and its affiliation of liberty, agriculture, and wealth. Of course, these days devious persons who work in offices have managed to divert the stream of wealth so that hardly any of it trickles back to the farm— not the wealth that is reckoned in dollars, anyway. But if the dollars are sparse, I still have a cupboard full of dried tomatoes to carry me through the year. And a bag of those tomatoes looks quite similar to a bag of coins and, being edible, is more useful. I reckon I'm fairly compensated.

Bad Day

We have been 171 days without rain. Here it is November, and I am still irrigating. Everything is covered with dust—the leaves of trees, the roofs of houses, the spirits of the people. This morning I turned on the computer to check the weather forecast. A few days ago the weatherman predicted a big storm, which was supposed to arrive today. But as the date grew closer, he lost his courage. First it was "Rain, heavy at times;" then, "Rain likely"; now the forecast is "Chance of showers."

When I checked my e-mail, an image popped up on the screen of an idiotic man dressed in red, white, and blue bunting, deliriously happy over the victories of the Republicans in yesterday's election. I voted, too, but for the most part my candidates did not win. Perhaps democracy in this country is by now a complete failure, with elections openly for sale to the highest bidder. Even worse, democracy might be a success, and the election shows the true character of our people as they cast their votes for a violently exploitative attitude toward the planet and its creatures.

I took a pail and a spade and walked through the orchards, checking for gophers. Three caught in yesterday's traps. Twelve new sets of mounds. Two olive trees killed, bitten off at the base. Everywhere the forces of evil are in ascendancy.

In the third volume of *Capitalism and Civilization*, Fernand Braudel remarks, "There are always some areas that world history does not reach, zones of silence and undisturbed ignorance." That is where I long to live.

A few nights ago I had an extraordinarily vivid dream that I had moved to the Falkland Islands—not the main island, one of the uninhabited outer islands—and started a farm in a bleak and windy place where the crash of waves on rocks and the cries of sea birds were the only sounds. If it were not for my wife and daughters guiding me along a different path, I would not be here writing this. I would be out at the barn, packing a cargo container with seeds and spades and boots and well points and all the other things I might need on that little island. There I could pass my remaining days in undisturbed ignorance—conversing with penguins, and trading insults with seagulls, and taking counsel from the waves—out of reach of history.

Two days later: Well, I am not moving to the Falkland Islands, at least not just yet. Perhaps that wish was simply a reconnaissance of the southern pole of an old bipolar condition, or an avatar of Scottish ancestry longing for the moors of Skye. Maybe it was just a bad day. And yet, I don't want to devalue the impulse, for there is a large splinter of my splintery personality that would happily live in such a place.

From the beginning of human history until about one hundred and fifty years ago, almost no one lived more than an hour's walk from wilderness. You could rise early in the morning, put a few crusts in your pocket for nourishment, and set out on foot to spend a day in a wild place where the sounds of wind and water and the calls of birds were the only sounds. In such a place one's soul heals. Humans are both social and solitary animals, and we need both society and solitude to keep our sanity. The wild places are nearly gone, and most people have hardly any solitude left to them; an hour in the car commuting to or from work is all they get, and it is of poor quality. (This is why carpooling has never caught on; it is not the inconvenience of it so much as the loss of the last bit of solitude that makes people reluctant to give up their solo commute).

It is not always clear what constitutes solitude. To be alone in a crowd is a cliché. And to judge by Thoreau's voluminous journals, the whole time he was at Walden Pond he kept the lively company of an invisible companion to whom he was incessantly yakking.

From my place I can start before dawn and drive east for three and a half hours into the deserts of Nevada, head down a side road, and then along an old mining track until the road ends. I can park my truck and get out and walk up into the hills. But even there the experience is flawed; jets crease the sky half a dozen times an hour, and the intervals between distant gunshots are brief.

What I would like to do, and what would restore my spirit, is to spend one day a week on one of the outer islands of the Falklands—a true Sabbath.

On My Father's Farm

My father, weary of his situation in California, decided to move. He did not know where he wanted to move to, but he knew how to discover his own unconscious wishes. He pinned a large map of North America to the side of a shed and, with eyes closed, tossed a dart at it. Navigating according to his feelings of disappointment or happiness at where the dart landed, he found that his desire was to move to Ithaca, New York, where years before he had operated a small farm while he was a student at Cornell. And so he packed up his goods, and moved to Ithaca, and bought a farm on a south-facing slope, and planted an orchard. At the time, he was eight-two years old.

A few years passed before I visited my father in his new place. After finishing the fall planting on my farm in California, I caught a flight east, rented a car, and drove down to his farm near Ithaca. Snow was falling as I pulled into the driveway.

The door to his house was open. I stood in the doorway and called out, but there was no answer. In the first room—the kitchen—the tables and counters were stacked with books and dishes, intermixed. The floor was covered with maple leaves that had blown in through the open door, or maybe the window, which also was open. The second room, once a dining room, was traversed by a narrow path between piles of books and heaps of mail. Leaves had blown into this room, too. The third room was lined with bookcases; open books—face up, face down—were heaped up against them like snowdrifts. In a far corner my father sat in a chair, reading. Snowflakes spiraled in through an open window and landed on the page; he brushed them away with the back of his hand.

My father wore many layers of mismatched and misbuttoned clothing; pens stuck out of every pocket. I called his name, but he did not hear me; he was completely deaf. I walked to where I blocked the light falling on his page. He looked up in puzzlement. After a minute, he recognized me.

The book that my father was reading when I interrupted him was *The Bamboos of British India* (Calcutta, 1896). My father had started out as a farmer, and he ended up as a farmer, but in between, for thirty years, he was a professor of botany and a specialist in grasses. Eighty-five years old, disabled by a stroke, he would never go to India. He would never see any of those bamboos. He was reading the way an old black man in Mississippi sits on the porch of his shack and reads the Bible, ignoring the narrative, but taking comfort in the familiar weight of the book and the rhythm of the language. The eight thousand botany books in his house were my father's bibles, a record of astonishing creation. He read them for heft and cadence, not content.

When I was a child, my father's relationship to me was one percent companionship, two percent scolding, and ninety-seven percent neglect. I believe that was typical of the era. He had his preoccupations and I had mine. He once remarked to my sister that he liked plants much more than he liked people. I'm sure that was true. He took far more delight from an unexpected trillium in the woods than he did from his own grandchildren. If we took a walk in the park, he would greet each bush and tree like an old friend, stroke it and groom it, pull off some dead leaves, pinch out a badly placed shoot. His hatband held sprigs of vegetation; his pockets were full of seedpods.

I had only a few days for my visit, and I used them to prepare for winter. I hitched a wagon to the tractor and hauled cordwood from a distant lot and stacked it by the house. I had the fuel oil tank topped up, although my father seldom used it. I took him shopping, bought him a warm hat, and stocked up the pantry for the winter. I carried cases of ale to the cellar, and a sack of potatoes.

In the sun porch of his house lay heaps of bulbs packaged for cut-rate retail, twenty-five tulips of a number-two grade in a plastic bag with a gaudy photo stapled to the opening. The bulbs were sprouting in their bags. There were more than a hundred bags of tulips, and other bulbs as well. On the last day of my visit the ground thawed, and I planted bulbs.

My father took some of the small bulbs—chionodoxa and crocus—and began arranging them on the front lawn. He laid out sticks, some curved, some straight, in an arcane pattern and placed the bulbs at the intersections. I took charge of the tulips. I would stick a spade in the ground, push it back to make a crescent shaped opening, and dump in half a dozen bulbs, then pull out the spade and close the hole with the heel of my boot. But I kept digging up daffodil bulbs, and peony roots, and oriental poppies, and who knows what else. There was no unoccupied ground. And so I drifted away from the house out into the pasture, spading open holes, and throwing in handfuls of tulips, and kicking the soil over the opening. It was fully dark when I dug a large hole, dumped the last seventy-five tulips into a mass grave, and covered them.

That winter I got disturbing phone calls from Ithaca. A neighbor called and said that my father had gone to his mailbox, twenty feet from his house, and become lost. He had stood for hours, peering anxiously up and down the road, until someone guided him home. A social worker had stopped to check on him and found him walking barefoot in the snow, wearing only a bathrobe, and carrying an axe over his shoulder. I made arrangements to have him moved to a place where he could be looked after.

The next spring my brother and I flew east to clean up my father's farm and get it ready to sell, and to find a good home for *The Bamboos of British India* and its eight thousand cousins. One afternoon we picked up my father and took him back to the old place. I don't think he knew who we were, or where he was. He walked slowly around the garden, his hands clasped behind his back, studying the plants. He gazed for a long time at the drunkard's path of scarlet tulips that angled across the pasture. In the front yard the sticks he'd laid out the previous fall were still in place. He recognized them, recognized that pattern that had meaning only to him.

Kneeling by the sticks, he put his face close to the ground, and in the way that one coaxes the embers of a reluctant fire by blowing very gently, he blew away some dried leaves, uncovering a pale, upward-tending shoot.

The Masters in the Trees

Human beings are one of those species of mammal that forms social hierarchies. This is achieved by pairwise confrontations in which one of the pair is determined to outrank the other. It is not as important to be found superior or to be found wanting as it is to know where one stands. And so we have deep within our genes a fundamental need to be judged.

When I was thirteen years old my father drove me in the old green Dodge down to the railroad station and asked the station master to flag down a train called *The City of San Francisco*. The train pulled into the station, a door opened, and I climbed aboard with my cello and suitcase and headed off to boarding school in Massachusetts, three thousand miles away.

The school I attended was an archetype of the fine old New England prep school. Sited atop a hill, its handsome brick buildings in the Georgian style were widely set on spacious lawns, connected by avenues of elms. My classmates were the sons of diplomats and New York bankers. They moved easily in the world of privilege; they could command servants, and order dinner in French, and distinguish a Ferrari from a Lamborghini. I had only just learned to tie a necktie, and half the time that came out wrong.

The teachers were referred to as masters and addressed as "Sir." It took me about a year to figure out that in spite of the tweed jackets with leather elbow patches, bulging briefcases, wire-rimmed glasses, and pipes of aromatic tobacco, they were a less-than-distinguished lot: failed academics, closet alcoholics, uninspired poets, and minor bullies of various species. And the students, except for a few truly gifted ones, were only marginally more clever than the field run of humanity. But the myth of school excellence was to everyone's advantage, and no one challenged it.

We took our meals in the dining commons, four spacious halls paneled in golden oak. One of the masters ate with us in each hall to keep an eye on things, and to quell riots. I remember once we were conducting an experiment to see how many saltine crackers one could fit into his mouth without breaking any. Ben Barker had about eleven in when someone made a humorous remark. Tears appeared in Ben's eyes, his face began to quiver, and then with a roar he spewed a comet of cracker crumbs forty feet across the room. The master got wearily up from his chair and came over to bawl us out. Not that he cared, but the infraction was too egregious to overlook.

In addition to the living masters, we were permanently scowled at by former masters, now dead, whose portraits hung in the dining halls, alternating with the Palladian windows around the outer wall of the room. These paintings must have been dark to begin with, and they had darkened even more over the years, until the canvases were nearly all black, except for the ghostly and disapproving faces.

I attended the school on a full academic scholarship, one privilege of which was the opportunity to show my gratitude by working twenty hours a week in the school kitchen. (Only years later did it occur to me that the scholarship was bogus; they were getting a half-time employee for less than minimum wage). Often I took my meals alone at an earlier hour than my classmates so that I would be free to operate a dish-washing machine during dinner.

One morning, walking alone at an early hour to my duties in the kitchen, I came around a corner and was astonished to find the portraits of the masters hanging on the trunks of a row of linden trees that marked the perimeter of a courtyard. Someone had broken into the commons during the night, removed the paintings, and rehung them, quite neatly, on the trees. Shadows of leaves played across the canvases in the early morning sunlight. I was seized with a feeling of irrepressible happiness, and felt that I had in one stroke gained some important and fundamental knowledge, though I could not have said what it was.

A special assembly was called that morning. The headmaster grimly condemned the outrage. It was disrespectful of the school's property (the cheap buggers hadn't insured the paintings and had been given a scare). And it showed a failure of citizenship in the wider school community (a lucky thing some wealthy potential donor didn't stumble on this and change his mind). Then the dean of students got up and said that if any boy had knowledge of this, it was his duty to report it to the dean (they had no clue who had done it). Severe disciplinary measures would be taken, and the culprits would be expelled, or worse.

That "or worse" hung in the air. The school's rules were set forth in a little booklet with a blue cover, and the mileposts on the path to damnation were clearly marked. Expulsion was not the worst; beyond expulsion lay expungement. The student who was expunged was not only expelled, but his name was removed from all school records, and the school would deny any knowledge of him. "Had anyone ever been expunged?" we wanted to know. "Yes, once, years ago."

"What did he do? What did he do?" We were giddy with curiosity about the magnificently twisted act that had led to expungement. But the secret was well kept. I suspect that in some way he had lifted the hem of those solemn academic robes to expose the weak flesh underneath.

I did not see the al fresco art festival as disrespectful. Quite the opposite. It seemed an act of kindness, like bundling an invalid relative into his wheelchair and taking him for a stroll in the garden. And I now realize that the perpetrators anticipated by three decades modern critical concerns with the contextuality of art, and did so not with tedious knots of five-syllable words, but by a bold and original act.

I had forgotten the incident of the masters in the trees for thirty-five years or so, and then one day it came back to me. I was standing in the hall of the farmhouse, talking on the phone. One wall of the hallway is hung with photographs of our extended family—a sort of rogue's gallery of ancestors. Across from me was a small portrait of my mother's great-uncle Michael, for whom I was named. The picture shows a solemn lad of about fourteen years old, wearing a baggy shirt and trousers and canvas boots, standing beside an ornately carved chair on which one hand rests. He came to this country as a penniless immigrant and started out selling produce from a pushcart. But he was intelligent and industrious, and rose in the business world, and eventually was elected president of the chamber of commerce in New Haven, Connecticut. For years his image had stood in the same spot; he looked out at a view of a telephone and a rolodex and some phone books, and it was while I was thinking about his view that I remembered the paintings in the trees. I had to turn off irrigation in the apricot orchard; I would take him for a walk. When my phone call was finished I picked up his photo and popped it into my shirt pocket, so that just the face looked out.

I stepped out onto the veranda. "Those mountains over there are the Coast Range, and just over the hill is the Napa Valley," I said. "Beyond that are a few more ranges and valleys, and then the Pacific Ocean." We walked down an avenue of olive trees. I pointed out the six acres of raised beds where we grow flowers, and the vegetable plot where young plants of fennel and radicchio had just been set out, and the well-tended orchard of plums belonging to my neighbor. I pointed out where our land ended at an apple orchard, half a mile away.

And then an astonishing thing happened. My mother's great-uncle Michael spoke to me. "I don't get it," he said. "Why are you doing this? Why are you scratching away in the dirt like a peasant? You had a fine education. You could have been a surgeon, or an engineer, or a scholar. You're just throwing away your life."

"I did start out to be a scholar," I said. "But it was mostly by way of fulfilling other people's expectations of me. I always felt like an imposter. It seemed to me, when I gave that up—with a considerable feeling of relief—and got into farming that I had found my destiny."

"That is preposterously self-indulgent," he said. And then he spoke no more. I shut off the irrigation in the apricots and we walked back to the house in silence. I replaced my mother's great-uncle Michael on his shelf.

I have grown accustomed to being a disappointment to my family; it's part of the curse of having been a promising child. At least I know where I stand. But in the case of my mother's great-uncle Michael, his disapproval of my choice of career shows mostly how much the world has changed. For centuries, to tend a little plot of land was the fate of most of humanity, and most were ill-suited to it, and so it was looked upon as drudgery, to be escaped from if at all possible. Now hardly anyone is left who can live a comfortable life by operating a tiny farm. Now we recognize what a rare privilege it is.

Joe Dvorak

PEOPLE WHO ARE SHORT AND WIRY OFTEN AGE BETTER than bulkier people do. That was the case with Joe Dvorak, who at eighty-six years old was by far the oldest farmer in the market, but was still spry and clear-witted. He was always one of the earliest to arrive at market, nosing his ancient Toyota truck into its spot and setting up his table of onions and garlic and gladioli and squash and whatever other oddments of produce he might have. Joe always dressed the same: a khaki jump suit and high top sneakers and a baseball cap and a red bandana tied around his neck. He had an old black dog named Pete; Pete wore a red bandana around his neck, too. Joe didn't sell a great deal; I think that as much as anything he was there to flirt with the ladies. From his perspective, a woman of sixty was a young thing, and they seemed to enjoy his attention.

I had known Joe most of my life. When I was a child the Dvoraks were neighbors of ours, and I used to work for them on Saturday mornings, mowing the grass and weeding the flower beds. In those days, Joe was a civil engineer, a specialist in bridge building. He was married to Mercedes. He had met her in Costa Rica when he was building a bridge there, and he had brought her back to California as his bride. They had three daughters, all older than me.

Most of the houses in our neighborhood had been put up by builders without much thought, but the Dvorak's house was designed by an architect, and it was a handsome building with expanses of glass and exposed wood. Mercedes had an unfailing eye for the decorative arts, and everything in their house was hand-made—ceramics, textiles, rugs, furniture, light fixtures, metal work. It was all beautiful, and all harmoniously arranged, and you could sense it immediately when you stepped in the door. In our backward little town it would not have been difficult to be a leader in the arts, but I think that Mercedes' exquisite taste would have been noticed even in San Francisco or Pasadena.

It was some years after my stint as a gardener for the Dvoraks, when I was home from college on a brief visit, that I heard that they were not getting along. Joe had quit his job as an engineer and moved out to some rural land that they owned, and was living in an old shed with a dirt floor and no electricity. There were vague hints of a mental breakdown. He had wanted Mercedes to move out there with him, and she was horrified by the prospect and would not go. A year or two after that, I was again in town on a visit, and I heard that they had divorced, and that Mercedes had moved back to Costa Rica, where her family still lived, though she was often in California visiting her daughters.

I became reacquainted with Joe after I had returned to the region and taken up farming myself. We often chatted at the market. One day he invited me to visit his place, and the following Sunday I drove out early, finding my way through a maze of gravel roads in the backcountry. Joe had forty acres of good, flat land, but he farmed only two acres. The rest he was restoring to its original vegetation, an oak savanna. He had planted valley oaks, and native grasses, and redbuds, and toyons. He'd had a pond dug in the low corner, and he was able to keep it filled through the dry season by running a little gasoline pump and taking water from the district ditch that ran along one edge of his place. Tules and cottonwoods grew at the edge of the pond, and ducks swam quietly among the reeds. Joe had put up nesting boxes for owls and bluebirds and tree swallows and bats, and the place was alive with birds and snakes and rabbits.

"I grow all my own food," said Joe. "The only thing I buy is coffee and salt and candied ginger. That little patch of wheat, about fifty by a hundred feet, is enough to make bread for a year. I bake bread on Mondays"—he motioned toward a wood-fired brick oven under a tree—"eight loaves, one for each day and one extra. I don't put anything up in jars, but I dry a lot in the sun—tomatoes, apricots, nectarines, squash, pears, peppers. And I have fresh fruit and vegetables all year-round. After the stone fruits we have persimmons, and then citrus comes in through the winter, and the grapefruits carry over into cherry season. It's amazing how much food comes out of two acres. It could easily feed thirty people. I sell some at the market, but mostly I give it to the food bank."

Joe offered me a cup of coffee, and I accepted. He got a little fire going and put a blackened pot of water on to boil. "I cook outside on a fire, year-round," he said. "If it's raining, I make a fire under the overhang."

When the coffee was ready Joe poured out two cups, and we sat down in a couple of aluminum lawn chairs under the valley oak that also shaded the little shed where he slept. We sat quietly for a while, sipping our coffee. Then I said, "So Joe, how is it that you went from being a family man and a civil engineer to leading this life? There must be an interesting story there. I'd like to hear it, if you'd care to tell it."

"Sure," said Joe. "It started in Colorado. I mean, it must have started long before that, but it began to take shape in Colorado. I'd gone out there to survey for a bridge. There was a new road going way back into some canyon lands—beautiful, quiet, pristine country. One evening I was sitting on a big rock at the edge of the stream that we were going to bridge, and I got to thinking about how once the bridge was built, the whole place would fill up with a bunch of jerks driving four-wheel drives and pulling trailers with snowmobiles and dirt bikes. They'd bring in cases of beer and throw trash all over and bring in guns and shoot up everything. And all of a sudden I had an insight that my whole career had been a terrible mistake. I had always thought about bridges as a kind of art, and I was very caught up in making a graceful bridge. The difference between a graceful bridge and a clumsy bridge is subtle, but it was very important to me. And I was so focused on the technicalities of bridge building—the equations of stress on a curved beam and all that—that I hadn't really stopped to think about the consequences of these bridges, which were, in fact, to facilitate the destruction of the world's last wild places. It seems obvious enough now, but until then it hadn't occurred to me. Kind of a blind spot there. I felt terrible, but I had no doubt about the correctness of my insight. After I came home I went into the office in Sacramento and turned in my resignation. I was eight months short of fifty-five, which is retirement age, and the boss was very good about leaving my name on the books for those eight months so I could get my pension.

"There was another thing going on in my life about the same time. There were some particularly lurid murders in the news, and I was getting very depressed by them. For years I read the newspaper every morning and evening, and listened to the news on the radio and on TV. I thought I was being a good citizen. Actually, it made me feel terrible. An endless chronicle of greed and stupidity and senselessness. And the reporters would be so proud when they discovered some new outpost of human depravity. I think that in following the news what I was really doing was sitting down five times a day and eating a big bowl of poison. It was poisoning me, that news. One night when it was particularly gruesome, I decided that I would never look at it again. And I haven't.

"I had bought these forty acres out here some years before as an investment, and I decided that instead of having someone farm it, I would restore it to its original state—the state it was in before people started messing with it. An act of atonement. Atonement for my career. I like to think of a bird flying high up, looking out over this whole valley of farmland, and then it spots my place, wild and forested, with a pond, and it thinks, 'That's where I'll go.' People ask me if I'm interested in habitat restoration. I'm not interested in it in general; I'm interested in it in specific, for this piece of land. I've shrunk my world down to this forty acres, and I don't worry anymore about what's outside its borders.

"After the girls left home, life with Mercedes changed. She was increasingly becoming an art collector—ceramics. It preoccupied her; it was on her mind all the time. She went to every show and gallery and studio, and never came home empty-handed. The house was just filling up with artifacts, and I felt like I was suffocating, my spirit was suffocating. There used to be a time, long ago, when I went to gallery openings full of enthusiasm and curiosity, to see what new marvels the human imagination could produce. But something changed there, too. Toward the end, I would go to an opening, and all I could think was, 'These poor lumps of clay, why must they be so burdened with the ego of the artist? All this striving for novelty and originality is so wearying and pathetic!' I got to where I couldn't stand it. I still like antique ceramics, though. Partly because of their age and their history and their simplicity, but mostly I like them for their anonymity. They can simply be themselves, without having to prop up the persona of some wretched artist. I now own just two plates and two cups and two bowls, an iron skillet, and a pot with a lid, and all of them are more than two hundred years old. That's one of those cups that you're holding there. I get a lot of satisfaction from them.

"Anyway, I was just extremely out of alignment with the world. Midlife crisis, I guess you could call it. I felt that somehow the way to make it right was to change my life, abandon all those ties, and try living in utter simplicity."

"And was that the right thing to do?" I asked. "You seem content."

"I miss Mercedes. I wish she had changed along with me, but instead we grew in different directions. And I missed music. Baroque, classical, sacred music. It had always been part of my life. I don't have electricity here. I could get it, but I choose not to. But a year ago I had a CD player put in my truck, and I can listen to music for three or four hours without running down the battery too badly. The acoustics are terrific. On a rainy winter day I'll sit in the cab of the truck half the day, listening to Bach.

"My daughters come around sometimes," he said. "They're good girls. They come to visit and bring the grandkids. I know that the older two think I'm nuts, but the youngest one seems sympathetic to my situation. And the grandkids love it here. They're young enough not to judge. There's always good fruit, and they can chase Pete into the pond and have a hell of a good time."

The morning was getting late, and I had chores to do at home. I thanked Joe for the visit and the story, and took my leave. Joe wouldn't let me get away without an armload of Stockton red onions and yellow squash, and an invitation to come again on a rainy day, when we could sit in the truck and listen to Bach.

Sometimes, at a dinner party, when the plates have been cleared away but the people are still at the table, talking, swirling wine around in glasses, sipping coffee, the story of Joe and Mercedes will come up in conversation. The women at the table cluck and nod among themselves. Most agree that it was tragic that Joe had a mental breakdown and quit his fine job, and outlandish of him to expect Mercedes to leave her beautiful house and go live in a hut with a dirt floor. They might point out, too, that an attack of mental illness in a husband was less humiliating for the wife than if he had run off with another woman. This is the drift of the women's conversation. The men don't say much, because we know the truth, and the truth is more subversive than the version of the story that the women prefer to believe. The truth is that among the breeds of domestic animals, the human male is the most tenuously domesticated. No matter how cozy the hearth whereby he sits, his feral self always naps with one eye open, looking longingly through an open doorway at a distant, wild land. The men know that Joe did not have a mental collapse. What he had was a fit of lucidity, and he had the courage to follow it. We regard with him admiration, and a trace of envy.

The Farmer Bakes a Cake

THE HAPHAZARD FLINGING TOGETHER OF GENES at the moment of conception stamps us with talents and deficiencies that endure for the rest of our lives. My sisters inherited a knack for cooking (genes which had been latent for a few recent generations). They can saunter around the kitchen, tossing ingredients together in a seemingly random and unpremeditated way, and create the most exquisite dishes, and they can scatter them onto a plate so artfully that it seems an act of vandalism to disturb the composition with your fork.

I have not got that knack. It's not that I am one of those pathetic males who subsists for eight days on cold canned spaghetti while his wife visits distant relatives. I can cobble together a decent plate of food—romaine drizzled with lemon juice and olive oil, sardines, linguini with pesto, and a bottle of chianti classico, thank you very much. But when I stray from my few well-worn culinary paths, I tend to get into trouble. So the kitchen is, by and large, the domain of my wife and daughters.

I don't feel inferior because of this. I have other skills: I can judge timber, and fell a tree, and start a fire, and shingle a barn, and fix a leaking toilet. These, and a few other talents that I can't recall at the moment, allow me to earn my keep around the place and hold my head high.

At one time I thought I might have an aptitude for baking, like my brother, whose deft, floury hands can shape all sorts of wonderful cookies and tarts. He makes bread dough so elastic that I can imagine holding an edge of it against the floor with my right foot, stretching it over my head with my left hand, and strumming the bass line to "Body and Soul." I tried to make bread, but the yeast at our place suffers from manic-depressive disorder. One batch of dough would lie sullenly in its bowl, face to the wall, sulking. The next time you'd catch it in a manic phase. Leave the room for a minute, and when you came back it had climbed out of the bowl and across the table and down to the floor, looking for a party. I baked a sweet potato pie one time and managed to fit eighteen large sweet potatoes—about half a bushel—into a nine-inch pie. It was astonishingly dense, calling to mind a lead brick I once tried to pick up at the Cambridge cyclotron.

On the morning in question I was rummaging around in the kitchen and came across a heart-shaped baking pan, which reminded me that the next day was Valentine's day, and I had the happy notion of baking a heart-shaped cake for my valentines, who were off on a shopping expedition. I got down *The Joy of Cooking,* which, like most everything else around our place, is fifty years out of date. It's the 1943 edition, with appendices describing how to send food to the troops overseas and how to cope with meat rationing. Our stove dates from the same era—a six-burner monster with more chrome than a Buick.

I started in on a recipe for white cake, which seemed simple enough. I was part way along with mixing the ingredients when I glanced out the window at the sun and remembered that I had covered some little citrus trees against a threatened frost. So I abandoned the kitchen for a moment, pulled on some boots, and hiked down to the orchard to uncover the trees. On the way back I noticed that weeds were coming up in a bed of two thousand Duke of Wellington tulips. I started weeding the bed, and I got to thinking about a girl named Linda whom I had admired from a distance thirty-five years ago. She played the French horn, and must have been a terrific kisser, but I never found out—I was too shy to talk to her. I was regretting how youth is wasted on the young when I remembered that I was in the midst of baking a cake. I laid off weeding and went back to the house.

The next ingredient to be added was two cups of flour, sifted twice. I've always thought that sifting flour was an absurd affectation;

I just dumped it in. I continued pretty well until I came to the instruction to add a cup of prunes. Prunes? What the hell? I studied the page. I was deeply embedded in the text of a recipe for prune cake. I flipped through the chapter and found my white cake recipe two pages back. When I was out weeding the tulips, the pages must have malevolently turned themselves. I compared the recipes, but there were irreconcilable differences. Should I add them up and divide by two, perhaps? Half a cup of prunes? No, that was ridiculous. But perhaps I would add some ginger, as a distraction, and some orange peel. I believe orange peel to be the solution to many culinary problems, sort of the way Catholics fix things up with a volley of *Ave Marias.*

The cake was not a success, although the gesture was appreciated. My wife politely ate a small piece, and over the next couple of days my daughters ran their fingers through the frosting. I decided to feed the remains to the birds.

There was an unusually large covey of quail around the place at that time—more than twenty birds. The male of the species has a feather shaped like a question mark quivering over his head, which shows him to be a less profound existentialist than his eastern cousin, who sports an exclamation point. The quail trek several times a day along a path that skirts a hedge of flowering quince, and this is where I scattered the crumbs. I didn't see the quail, but when I checked the next day, every crumb was gone.

Subsistence

In a fine little book called *Soil and Civilization* by Edward Hyams (not to be confused with *Topsoil and Civilization* by Vernon Carter) the author remarks, "It is possible to grow cash crops in the spirit of subsistence agriculture." That aptly describes my style of farming. Although most of what we grow is intended for sale, money is not what's on our minds. Our citrus grove can serve as an example.

A couple of times a year I spend an afternoon at the university library reading agricultural journals. I read them all, and if they are written in a language that I don't understand, then I look at the pictures and study the advertising. On one of these afternoons I was reading a little citrus-industry newsletter called "The Citrograph." The lead article was about clementine mandarins. The author pointed out that they were immensely popular; that there was hardly any domestic production, nearly all the crop being imported from Spain; and that there were almost no organic clementines available at all. It looked like an obvious opportunity. There is already an industry of mandarin culture in my district, but the crop is almost entirely a variety called Owari Satsuma; no one grows clementines.

If I had the mentality of a cash crop farmer, I would meet with the agricultural extension agent for citrus, and I would meet with produce brokers and try to set up a contract, and I would meet with my banker. I would calculate very carefully the capital cost for the orchard and for irrigation, and compare amortization of a well on twenty versus thirty acres. I would try to predict global production based on nonbearing acres currently planted. I would estimate the costs of labor and spraying and management, and the costs of borrowing money. The banker and I might figure out that the crop would break even in the eleventh year and by year twenty would yield a net return on investment of eight point seven percent. A twenty-page business plan would be typed up. Lawyers would be brought into the picture, and contracts and agreements would be signed. This is the modern way of engaging in farming; an accountant with an MBA would be happy with it.

I don't think that way. In our location, clementines are ready to harvest in January, a month in which ordinarily we have no income, and hardly any chores, so clementine culture would fit well into our schedules. I called around and found that the nurseries selling the trees were all about four hundred miles away, and none of them made deliveries. The trees are heavy, and it would be pushing it to fit a hundred of them into my van. If I made two trips, which is as much driving as I would feel like doing in one month, that would be two hundred trees. This determined the size of my orchard. It also would fit my budget; since I don't use credit, I have to work within the scope of my savings. I don't use hired labor, either, and I figured that as the trees reached maturity, allowing for rainy days, I might be able to pick about five thousand pounds of fruit each January. Losing the crop to a freeze two years out of five would leave me an average of three thousand pounds of fruit each year. I would sell a third of this at retail at eighty cents a pound; and another third at wholesale, at fifty cents a pound; and the rest would go to the food bank to feed the homeless. This would give me a gross income of thirteen hundred dollars a year. Ignoring amortization of the trees and pipeline, I would have annual expenses of organic registration ($75), organic certification ($350), irrigation water ($200), clover seed ($40), and irrigation repairs ($35), for a total of $700, leaving me $600 dollars of net income. Between mowing, tending irrigation, setting gopher traps, and harvesting the fruit, I might spend one hundred hours a year in labor. So the result would be a wage of six dollars per hour—seventy-five cents less than minimum wage—and no return at all on investment.

The cash crop farmer looking at these figures would throw down his pencil and say, "Forget about citrus, it doesn't pay." But my interpretation is a little different. As I see it, by growing my two hundred trees of clementines, I would have an extra six hundred dollars of income in January instead of no income at all. Undoubtedly that would be helpful in getting us through a tough month. And because I make no distinction between work and play, the amount of labor is irrelevant. If I weren't taking care of the citrus, I'd have to find something else to do with my time. Indeed, to spend one's days walking in a handsome grove of aromatic trees liberally hung with golden fruits is for many people a vision of paradise. As I see it, the wage is superfluous.

Postscript: As it turns out, my estimate of yield was way off. With the trees coming into maturity the yield exceeds fifteen thousand pounds, not five thousand.

Perfect Tomato

THERE IS NO GREATER PLEASURE on a stormy winter evening than to sit in a comfortable chair in front of the fire with a stack of seed catalogues, the way a sensualist settles down with his *Playboy* and *Penthouse*. Look at this unblemished skin, radiant as if lit from within (I'm talking about a tomato). Or here, where the low angle of the light illuminates a fine fuzz of downy hairs disappearing around a plump curve into the shadow of an alluring cleft (I'm talking about a peach). And look at this turgid morsel of luminous pinkness; one could fairly lick the page (I'm talking about a raspberry). Such entertainment seems harmless enough, except that there is a subtle risk: the unthoughtful reader might come to believe that the flawless image on the glossy page is genuine.

The perfect tomato of the seed catalogue, and the digitally primped Miss January, are fictions, so convincingly presented that one might believe in their reality. And believing that, one then looks around at the tomato on the table and the woman sitting in front of it, and it seems that they fall short. In this view, every tomato, irregular and eccentric, scarred by the vicissitudes of its history, is a failed attempt at the tomato of the seed catalogue, in the same way that a woman who looks interesting is a failed attempt at Miss January. One imagines the judges holding the scorecards over their heads: 7.8, 7.2, 7.6, out of a possible ten.

A customer who, having been seduced by the glossy page, holds this view of the world is frustrating to the farmer. Such a one looks contemptuously at the farmer's offering of tomatoes, deigns to run his thumbnail across one, and then walks off without buying anything. Perhaps he is a tax auditor who believes th""t the word "tomato" written on a scrap of paper is more real than the tomato itself. After he marries Miss January, the two of them can select perfect tomatoes directly from the video screen.

The notion of a perfect tomato is part of the centuries-old dispute between Platonism and pluralism. Plato suggested that our perceptions are like shadows cast by a flickering fire onto the rough walls of a cave, and that there exists an object of perfection, whose shadows we observe, that we can never quite apprehend. In the opposing camp of the pluralists, the best-known champion is William James, a man so wise that he could knowingly hold contradictory views simultaneously and still sleep well at night. His book *A Pluralistic Universe* was published in 1908, at a time when pluralism had the advantage. For at that time, the technology of reproducing images was so poor that much was left to the imagination, and the farmer, guided by a crude copperplate engraving in his seed catalogue, likely felt that most any tomato came close enough.

Now Platonism has the upper hand. The proliferation of digitally tuned electronic images is unstoppable—one can hardly escape them—and a generation is coming of age that has known the glossy perfection of the electronic universe since infancy. Reality, by comparison, is a bit tattered, threadbare in places, and here and there misshapen and miscolored, and off the beat and out of tune. To those of us surviving pluralists, the irregularity of reality is a treasured and endearing trait. We look with uneasiness at the neoplatonists, who, like the neoconservatives in politics, are an alien and scary race.

April 2

Sixty bunches of tulips to the co-op
Sixty bunches of tulips to Nugget
Weed the ranunculus beds
Set gopher traps in the peonies
Start melons in the greenhouse
Start gourds
Transplant sunflower seedlings
Sow six more flats, sunflowers
Start seeds: zinnias, helichrysum,
    celosia, marigolds, atriplex
Plant out tomato seedlings
Mow in the olive orchard
Work up beds, south field
Repair flat tire
Pay dues — watershed coalition
Renew spray permit for olives
Final planting of gladiolus: 3,000 bulbs
Cut back forsythia
Repair leaking water valves
Irrigation Technology — get drip tape,
    pressure regulators
Chip apricot prunings
Cut fallen eucalyptus for firewood
Stake lilies
Order rubber bands
Order chrysanthemum cuttings

Bouquet of Flowers

IN FAIRY TALES, THE COBBLER'S CHILDREN GO UNSHOD, and the lawyer dies without a will, and one might think that, by analogy, as a flower grower I would have no flowers on my table. But that is not true. There are always some flowers that are unsold that find their way into the house, and often I am evaluating new varieties, and so have them in a vase. Then too, my daughters sometimes gather flowers for their own amusement, and bring them to the table. And rarely, in a whimsical mood, I gather a bouquet for myself.

The flowers I gather for myself are humble ones: the flowering panicles of little native grasses, unripe seed pods, perhaps a shoot of burr oak, with its oddly shaped leaves, a wild poppy from which the petals have already fallen. It is a botanist's bouquet, in shades of green, better appreciated through a lens—a bouquet meant for close inspection and contemplation.

Early on in the flower business I made bouquets like this to take to market. I thought that these humble little flowers and pods were so subtle and delightful that others would appreciate them too. I was wrong. In the marketplace, nothing succeeds like excess. A flaming red peony the size of a dinner plate is what people are after. If a customer noticed the subtle bouquet at all he would stare at it in puzzlement, as if it were a strange mistake.

Once in a while I take a little green botanical bouquet to market. In the course of the evening several hundred people come by my stand, and there might be one, sometimes not, who appreciates what

I am up to. It is always a quiet person who picks up that bouquet, studies it at close range, and says, softly, "I'll take this one. How much is it?"

I lay the bouquet diagonally on an open sheet of the *Wall Street Journal* and roll it up into a neat cone and hand it to her. "There's no charge," I say. The bouquet wasn't meant for commerce. Rather, it was like the glass slipper, or the pea under the mattress—a means of discovering a kindred soul.

Good Weed

ONE DAY I WAS IN THE FARMERS' CO-OP, picking up some fertilizer, when I spied a note on a bulletin board offering a Farmall Super-C tractor for sale. I make a point of checking out old tractors for sale, not because I intend to buy them, but because I always learn something talking to other farmers about their equipment. I copied down the number and phoned them when I got home. Only after I wrote down the directions did I realize that the seller was Good Weed Farm.

For years I had heard about Good Weed Farm, but I had never been there. I had heard that it was an organic hippie commune tucked into a little valley back in the hills. I had heard that the communists advocated free love, and went around naked, and had wild orgies. I had heard that exchange of mates was so casual that when children were born in the commune they knew who their mothers were, but paternity was always speculative. And I had heard that the good weed celebrated in the name of the farm was neither a dandelion nor a thistle. These rumors I neither believed nor disbelieved.

The workers from Good Weed who came to the farmers' market seemed to belong to that sect of organic farmers who disdain washing. They wore muddy clothes and had muddy feet, and favored a hairstyle of matted dreadlocks interwoven with beads and feathers. But they did their jobs well, and their produce was always excellent, though high priced.

One afternoon I drove out through the backcountry, from time to time consulting the instructions I had written on a scrap of paper, until I came to a sign that read "Good Weed Farm." The gate was open. I drove in and followed the road back to a cluster of buildings. There was something odd about the place. Every fencepost and tree trunk and boulder was covered with drawings in colored chalk. Swirls and spirals and lively zoomorphic shapes were drawn in fuchsia and azure and yellow. I was reminded of the drawings of Joan Miró. And when I reached the buildings, I noticed that they too were covered with drawings up to a height of about five feet.

No one was in sight. At the second building the door was open, and I could see a boy about fourteen years old working at a computer. I stepped in. "Excuse me," I said. "I'm looking for John."

"Probably outside," said the boy. The computer screen was not a video game, as I might have expected, but lines of odd symbols.

"What are you working on there?" I asked.

"Writing some code," he said.

"What's it do?"

"It's supposed to provide iterative solutions to a class of differential equations. Sometimes it works."

"That's amazing," I said. "Did you learn about this in school?"

"I'm home-schooled," he said. "I figured it out myself."

"Are you going to go to college?" I asked.

"I'm thinking about Davis or Berkeley," he said. "Maybe next year."

"Those are good choices," I said. "You might check out MIT, too. I take it you're not going to go into farming."

He looked at me and laughed—just one short, contemptuous laugh, like a single bark from a dog. At that moment I saw an older man walk by outside, and I stepped out and called to him. It was John. He was about my age, graying and balding, walking with a bit of a limp. "Oh yeah, the Super-C," he said. "Over this way."

"So, do you do the farming here?" I asked.

"No," he said. "I take care of the equipment: tractors, trucks, cars, pumps, coolers, sprayers, heaters, you name it."

"Sounds like a full-time job," I said.

"At least."

The Super-C was a beautiful little tractor, well kept up, with two tool bars between the axles and two more out the back. It started right up, and ran without smoking. It was set up for sixty-inch beds; mine are forty-eight. "Why are you selling it?" I asked.

"We've gone to all-diesel tractors with enclosed cabs that have heat and air conditioning. CD players too. Makes it easier on the workers."

John gave me a tour of the farm. It was a beautifully laid out and well-kept place. I would guess there were thirty acres of vegetable crops on the flat ground and another eighty acres of vines and trees on the slopes. He also introduced to me some of the original commune members. They had the haggard look that one expects of farmers in their fifties. None of them was naked. I thanked John for the tour and said that I'd call him if I decided to pursue the Super-C.

As I came around the corner to where my truck was parked, I could see that it was covered with drawings in colored chalk—purple rattlesnakes on the tires, blue fish on the door. I surprised the artist at work. She was a girl, about eight or nine years old, wearing a long flowing skirt and a t-shirt. She had shining black eyes, and black hair pulled back in a bun—a little gypsy. When she saw me, she bolted, dashing swiftly up the hill, barefoot, a fat chalk in each hand, and ducked behind a tree. She looked out at me. "Thank you for decorating my truck," I called out. "It's beautiful! I love it! If you

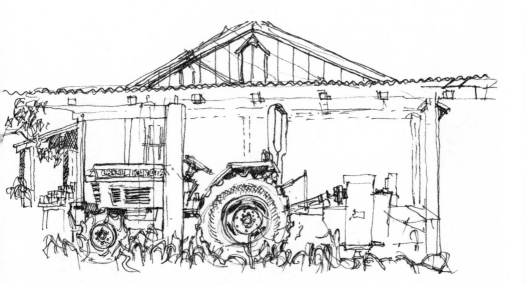

want to finish it, that would be great." But she must have suspected a trick, for she didn't come out from behind her tree. I headed for home.

If there ever were orgies at Good Weed, they must now be a thing of the past. There's something about bifocals and arthritis and fifty years of the tug of gravity on sagging flash that takes the charm out of it. Still, I like to think that it happened once, that one time a group of beautiful and healthy young people loosened the chafing strictures of social rules and cast them aside, and piled together in a happy, slippery mass, like seals on a rock. I have no regrets about not having been there myself; this is an experience which probably is best enjoyed vicariously, or in legend. When a few of the inmates escape, it's a victory for all of the prisoners.

Two Economies

Farmers often tinker with their lineup of equipment, trying to find a way to make life easier, and it was in such a mood that I decided that I needed a roller. What I had in mind was a fat steel cylinder two and a half or three feet in diameter and four feet wide that could be filled with water to give it some heft, and towed behind a tractor. I wanted it for firming the soil in my bulb beds. I plant about sixty thousand bulbs every year, and for planting I work up the beds so that the soil is fluffy and full of air. This is great for planting, but not so great for growing. Top-heavy flowers like gladioli are easily blown over if the soil is too loose. But more to the point, a gopher can swim through that loose soil eating the bulbs, and I won't know he's there. But if the bed is rolled firm, then the gopher has to throw up mounds of earth as he excavates his tunnels; these betray his presence, and I can trap him.

I went around to my equipment guy and told him what I was looking for. "Four feet wide," he said, rubbing his chin. "That's a problem. If you want a roller twelve feet wide, or fifteen feet, or twenty, I can have one in a couple of days, new or used. But four feet? I've never seen one. You'll have to have it custom built."

"Can you recommend someone to build it?" I asked. He gave me the names of a couple of equipment fabricators, and I went around to get estimates.

At the first place I went to, the staff parking lot was full of new, large pickup trucks with gun racks and American flags and patriotic bumper stickers. I parked my old flatbed and went inside. It was the usual sort of industrial shop—a big workroom full of equipment, and off to one side, offices with low ceilings and buzzing fluorescent lights and shabby furniture. Rush Limbaugh boomed his nonsense on the radio. "Yeah?" said the receptionist.

"I'd like to talk to an estimator," I said. I took a seat where she motioned me, under a calendar depicting hunters in camouflage clothing slung about with guns and knives and straps of bullets. After a while the estimator came—potbellied fifty-something—and gave me a dirty look. Maybe it was my wire-rim glasses and beard that made me look too much like a Green Party voter. We went to his office and I explained what I needed.

"That pipe comes in twenty-one-foot lengths," he said. "We can't buy just four feet; we have to buy a whole length. He made some sketches, and punched numbers in a calculator. "It would be about fourteen hundred dollars," he said. "Do you want me to write up the estimate?"

"How long would it take to do the work?" I asked.

"Six or eight weeks."

"Don't write it up just yet," I said. "I want to look into one other possibility first." I thanked him for his time, and told him I would call him if I wanted to go ahead with it. Then I made my escape.

The second place was similar: new big trucks, American flags, Rush Limbaugh on the radio, a surly estimator. "Seventeen hundred eighty-two dollars," he said.

I remembered an old machine shop on Highway 16 where I'd had some bushings made once. It was a tin shed set in the midst of two acres of junk tractors, and it was run by some scary-looking but jovial bikers. The office had a fascinating array of pornography taped to the ceiling, and when the manager was thinking, he rolled his eyes heavenward. He said, "We just do machining, not fabrication."

"Can you think of anybody who could do that for me? Maybe somebody out of the mainstream."

"You know," he said, "there's a blacksmith in a little town north of here. He might do it for you." He couldn't remember the name, but he told me how to get there. "There's only four streets in that town—it won't be hard to find."

I drove to the town; the smithy was on the third street. The owner was leaning against a walnut tree in front of his shed. He sized me up as I pulled in. I was driving my '86 Chevy with the bad paint, and my blue jeans had patches sewn over the knees. I think I passed muster. I greeted him, and he invited me in.

Inside, the shop was cool and dark. A couple of Mexican men were welding. An old forge, black with use, occupied the center of the room, and an enormous anvil was spiked to a stump. We talked in Spanish. I explained the kind of roller I needed, and pointed out that it required a long yoke because this particular tractor had a short draw bar. "What do you need it for?" he asked. I explained about the bulbs and the gophers, and the nature of my little farm. "I think we can do something," he said. "Let me get your phone number and I'll call you."

The next day he called. "I've located a four-foot length of used pipe thirty inches in diameter. It's quarter-inch steel—good, heavy stuff. He wants two hundred bucks for it."

"So how much would the whole roller come to?" I asked.

"I think four hundred dollars," he said.

"That's great," I said. "Let's do it."

Three days later, my roller was ready, and I went to pick it up. It was beautifully built. It rotated on an inch-and-a-half steel shaft mounted to the yoke with big bearings with zerk fittings. The welding was smooth and perfect. A crossbar on the yoke was positioned just a quarter-inch from the drum so that it could knock off any mud that stuck to the cylinder. There were plugs on each end, set 180 degrees opposite each other so that one could serve as a vent when the cylinder was being drained. One of the Mexicans, a man about forty, was standing there. "Did you build this?" I asked.

"Yes," he said.

"Thank you," I said. "It's a beautiful piece of work. Have you built these before?"

"No," he said. "This was the first one. I was lying awake one night, and got it laid out in my mind, and then I just came in and built it."

While the men were getting a forklift and putting the roller on my trailer, I paid the owner. "With the sales tax it's $429," he said. I pulled a wad of cash out of my shirt pocket and counted it out. We shook hands all around, and said our good-byes, and I went on my way. At home I had half a gallon of red enamel paint left over from when I had fixed up an old Farmall tractor, and I gave the roller a couple of coats. It looked great.

In my district, there are two economies. In one the people make sixty dollars an hour, and in the other they make ten dollars an hour. In the sixty-dollar economy, represented by the commercial fabricating shops I visited, you get a written estimate in triplicate. Once you sign the contract, you can be sure that the product will be as specified. The owners have licenses, and certificates, and permits, and bonds, and carry liability insurance. They belong to the Rotary Club and the chamber of commerce. You can open an account with them and have credit extended to you.

In the ten-dollar economy, there are no licenses or permits or certificates, no liability insurance, no chamber of commerce. Nothing is written down. Used materials and recycled parts are to be expected. The work is usually good, but it might be somewhat irregular. Payment is in cash. It helps if you speak Spanish or Vietnamese.

The ten-dollar economy works because it's based on honor. The players may be poor, but they are proud, and a handshake is all the contract that's needed. In the sixty-dollar economy, in place of honor there are written contracts and an abundance of lawyers.

(There's also a two-hundred-dollar-per-hour economy, in which words and numbers are sold, the flimsiness of the product shored up by the substantial price. In this economy the players smile at you broadly, showing all sixty teeth, while they slide your money into their pockets.)

Over the years I've been poor enough to have bought used tires instead of new ones for my truck, and to have debated whether I could afford to spend fifty dollars for a secondhand washing machine, and to have constructed buildings out of salvaged materials, and so I feel right at home in the ten-dollar economy. I have always found the people in that economy to be honorable. Well, almost always. In the off-season, I sometimes do day labor—roofing or carpentry. If the people appear to be wealthy I charge twelve dollars an hour, and if they're poor I charge five, and look for some opportunity for barter. Working in the ten-dollar economy is not just an economic issue—it is also social and political. It's a way that poor people have of outmaneuvering the wealthy parasites in the other economies.

Every time I walk past my roller I admire it. It is an unselfconscious piece of industrial art, simple and functional and well built. It works exactly as intended, and every fall and spring when I plant bulbs I roll the beds, making the bulbs comfortable, and the gophers uncomfortable. As much as anything, I like that the roller was made for me by someone who appreciated what I was up to, and who had the craftsman's pride to do beautiful work when something less would have sufficed. And I am pleased that no smarmy guy in an expensive suit made so much as a dime off the deal.

Pete

PETE WAS WELL PAST FORTY YEARS OLD, but he was still an under-graduate at the university. He would sign up for one course a semester and, as often as not, drop it before the semester was over. When he was in danger of graduating, he would change his major to stretch things out a few more years, and so he had changed from history to economics to art. He was at the university not so much to improve his mind as to meet women.

Pete lived in a little garage apartment with inexpensive rent, and earned a sort of living doing odd jobs—occasional bits of gardening, or painting, or light carpentry. He was handsome and tall, about six foot two, made taller by the motorcycle boots that he wore, and strong without that pumped look of those who lift weights and swallow steroids. When I saw Pete at the Wednesday night farmers' market, he was always accompanied by an attractive woman. Some of the women were demure; others were triumphant, as if they had been big-game hunting and bagged a trophy. He had figured out the perfect cheap date. He would bring two bottles of beer with him from home in a paper bag, so as not to have to buy from the local microbrewery at three dollars a glass. He and his companion would get tamales at the tamale stand and walk through the market to the park, where they could sit on the grass and listen to the band. When he passed my stand, Pete would wink and make a little motion with his hand, indicating that he wanted me to set aside a bunch of flowers that he would pick up later. I always make a few minimalist bouquets that sell for two dollars for the benefit of those whose budgets or interests extend only that far, and when Pete gave me the nod I knew to set one of these aside for him. At the end of the evening, Pete would come by and pick up the flowers and present them to his date. He had managed the whole evening—dinner, drinks, live music, and a bunch of flowers—for about eight dollars.

Every week he had a different woman. He was an equal-opportunity employer with respect to race, coloring, and stature as long as she was beautiful. Only once did I see him come through the market with the same woman a second time. She was petite, Asian, less than five feet two, with lovely dark skin and bushy eyebrows—Filipina perhaps. The first week she seemed as skittish as a doubtfully tamed colt—easily spooked, and ready to bolt. The following week she leaned dreamily against Pete, her arm around him and her hand in his back pocket, fully domesticated. The next week he was with a blond.

Pete drove a BMW motorcycle, the perfect vehicle for a serial seducer. His date, seated behind him, had to wrap her arms and legs around him and hold on tight for a bouncy and thrilling ride—a sort of mock copulation. And later in the evening, when he was facing the right direction, it was as if the precedent for lovemaking had already been set.

Pete's behavior reminded me of an alcoholic, someone who has found a pleasurable little step in life and is stuck there, repeating it over and over, somehow unable to progress beyond it. Never having been handsome or suave myself, I had experienced such smooth seductions only in my imagination, and so to some degree I envied Pete. But I also thought that there was something pathological about him, or at least immature. It was as if, having been told that the first bite of a peach is the best one, he had sat down with a bushel of peaches, taking one bite of each and throwing the rest away.

It occurred to me one Wednesday that I hadn't seen Pete in a few weeks, and when I asked around I heard that he had crashed his motorcycle and been badly injured. "Was there anyone with him?" I asked, thinking of those innocent women being hurled against the pavement, but there had been no one with him.

A couple of months later Pete came though the market. He was alone. I almost didn't recognize him. He carried a cane in his left hand, and walked with a gimp and a wince, all the swagger gone out of him. His hair seemed to have lost its luster, and there was a look of pain in his eyes. I came out from behind my table and shook his hand. "Pete," I said. "It's good to see you up and getting around. You had us worried there."

"Yeah," he said. "Had myself worried too."

"So how's it going?" I asked.

"One day at a time," he said. That's another thing that alcoholics are always saying. We talked a bit, and he went on his way. He looked to me like a man on the threshold of old age. A man who had no savings, no land, no house, no career, no wife, no children.

"Time to get on with it," I thought. "Time to graduate."

Bob Johnson

THE FIRST THING I NOTICED about Bob Johnson was not Bob him-self, nor the sweet corn and tomatoes he had for sale, but his truck, a 1961 Chevrolet so extraordinarily ugly that in a perverse kind of way it was attractive. What struck me about the truck was that it looked like it was brand new—fresh dark green paint, new tires, shiny chrome, no dings or scratches. I peered into the cab; the upholstery was new, a fire extinguisher was bolted to the frame, and a flashlight stood at the ready on the steering column. There was a custom-built canopy over the bed, with racks for carrying the mar-ket tables and umbrellas. The floor of the bed was a long shelf that rolled out on ball-bearing slides so that Bob could unload his truck comfortably while standing on the ground, instead of having to crawl in, grunting and swearing, like the other farmers do.

I got to talking to Bob about his truck. He told me that he'd had it for twenty-seven years, and that every fourth year, in the winter, he completely disassembled it, replaced any part that looked worn, painted the parts that took paint, and put it back together again. In another two years he'd do it for the seventh time. On winters of the intervening years he'd do the same for his other truck, an old GMC five-yard dump, and his two tractors, a Farmall Model M and a two-cylinder John Deere, so that each winter one machine got the treat-ment. I asked him if I could drop by sometime and see his tractors, and he said, "Sure." A few weeks later I went by his farm.

Bob's place was one of a group of little five-acre parcels that had been sold to Okies in the 1930s. It had the original house, and a barn, and several sheds and outbuildings. Bob, and his little dog, Sparky, showed me around. The cultivated land was divided into four equal parts, separated by fences. They were pasture, vegetables, one-year-old alfalfa hay, and two-year-old alfalfa hay. Each year, the two-year hay went to vegetable, the vacated vegetable ground went to pasture, and the old pasture was planted to alfalfa. The pasture had a small mixed flock of sheep and chickens. It was a good, sound farming system. Bob grew mostly summer vegetables—Early Girl and Beefsteak tomatoes, Silver Queen corn, Yolo Wonder peppers, and a miscellany of melons and cucumbers. Like his equipment, the varieties were from forty years ago.

"That's a great crop rotation," I said. "How did you come up with that?"

"Oh, my father laid out the fences and started that back about 1940. I've just kept it going."

The tractors were beautiful—steel sculpture of a useful kind. The Deere started with a single spin of the flywheel, making its characteristic popping sound. The tractors were kept in a shed with all manner of spare parts carefully arranged on shelves. Everything about the place was neat. Every bit of metal was freshly painted, every moving part was freshly lubricated. There was a metal-working shop with a lathe and a mill, and a woodworking shop. Various miniature buildings and bridges were under construction. Bob had fallen in with a bunch of guys who did model railroading, and he developed a knack for building the scale model buildings to go with their trains, and now he had commissions lined up years into the future.

"I retired a few years ago from my job as a lineman with the electric company," Bob told me. "I have a good pension; I just do the farming and the little buildings for something to do."

I have a big resaw bandsaw at my place, and I invited Bob to come by and use it when he needed to mill out very thin lumber for his buildings. He came by a few times, and we got to be friends in a casual sort of way. We'd talk at the farmers' market when things were slow. He was quiet and conservative, in the best sense of the word;

he believed in the enduring value of old things, and kept his equipment and buildings and land accordingly. His life had an orderliness to it that was attractive, in a monastic sort of way. I wondered idly about his private life; considered that maybe he was gay, maybe had lost weekends in San Francisco from time to time. He never mentioned any sort of mate.

A few years after I had met Bob, I was at one of my daughter's Saturday morning soccer games. Soccer played by seven-year-old girls is not all that interesting, and I got to talking with one of the other fathers, name of Doug. He told me that he was a lineman with the electric company.

"Maybe you know a friend of mine who used to be a lineman," I said. "Bob Johnson."

"Sure, I know Bob," he said. "We were partners for a long time. Not a guy to go out drinking with, and I don't think I ever heard him tell a joke, but when you're working high voltage you don't want a drinker and a joker, you want some guy that's solid as a rock. I liked working with Bob. How's he doing?"

"He's doing well, I believe. He's got a little farm, and builds tiny buildings for model railroads. But it seems like he doesn't have much of a social life. Maybe you know: did he ever have a girlfriend, or a boyfriend, or something like that?"

"Bob? Why, he's married."

"Really?" I said. "He's never mentioned it, and I've never seen any sign of a wife around there."

"Well, that's a story, it is." At this moment there was a cry from the crowd. A goal had been scored. "Go Megan! Go Blue Dolphins!" We waited for the shouting to die down. Over the course of the soccer game Doug related the story of Bob's marriage. His tale was kind of sketchy, and so I've supplied some missing details from my imagination.

"Cindi is her name. She was a dispatcher at the electric company. Good-looking girl, big mop of curly hair; some weeks she was a redhead, some weeks she was a blond. She wore short skirts and high heels, and she had a way of crossing her legs and winking at a man that would make him spill his coffee in his lap. She was a party animal; hard drinker, hard partier. Every night was Saturday night for

Cindi. I think she dated every lineman in the north state, and other guys too. I was already married when I transferred here, so I did not go out with her myself, but I wish I'd known her when I was single. She looked like she could suck the chrome off a trailer hitch. There was something sultry in her voice, too. She could say the most ordinary thing—'transformer out in the forty-two hundred block of Currey Road'—and you could imagine that while she said it she was unzipping her dress. I tell you, the guys kept their ears glued to that radio. She was a great dispatcher.

"Seems like Cindi got to a stage in her forties when life started catching up with her. She was just worn out. She was tired of getting up at four a.m. for an early shift. She was tired of her crummy little apartment, and her Trans Am, which was a piece of junk that broke down all the time. She was tired of creditors bugging her all the time for money. She wanted financial security, and peace, and untroubled sleep. She decided it was time to settle down, and she chose Bob, Mr. Sober, the complete opposite of all the guys she'd dated all those years. She knew from a girl over in accounting that he had more than five hundred thousand dollars in his 401k.

"One day Bob was in the office, filling out some papers, and Cindi struck up a conversation. She says, 'So what church do you go to, Bob?'

"Bob said, 'The First Baptist Church over on Road 29. How about yourself?'

"I don't believe Cindi had set foot in a church in thirty years. She said, 'Uh, the uh First Church of Christ, uh Covenant.'

"'I don't think I know that one,' he said.

"'It's in Vacaville,' she said. 'Actually, the preacher's kind of long-winded; I was thinking of finding a new church. Are you happy with your church, Bob?'

"'Why yes,' he said. 'I am.'

"That next Sunday, Bob's sitting in church, his usual place, and just as the music is starting, Cindi slips in beside him. She's wearing a pale blue suit, and blue shoes without too much heel, and she has her hair up, and she's cute as all get out. When it's time to sing a hymn she doesn't pick up a hymnal, she looks at his, kind of leans up against him. She doesn't know the words or the tunes, but she fakes along okay. When the service is over Bob gets up to go and she gets up and slips her arm through his and walks down the aisle like she was Mrs. Bob, and she had him, right there. He was a goner. I bet all those old biddies with unmarried middle-aged daughters who'd thought of him as a possible son-in-law and rejected him were kicking themselves. Because with Cindi on his arm, he suddenly looked very attractive.

"Bob asked Cindi out on a date: dinner at Denny's and a movie. It was a demure evening—no drunken sex in the cab of a pickup truck like she was used to. Then he took her out fishing one Sunday afternoon. And then he asked her to marry him.

"He hinted to her that her wedding present would be something automotive. She went out and test drove a green Lexus and a white BMW, and told him all about it. But as she learned on the wedding day, his present to her was to take her Trans Am completely apart and rebuild it, and paint it, and make it like new. She hid her disappointment well enough, I guess, and I believe that he was unaccustomed to the company of women and didn't pick up on any subtleties. So he worked on that car and got it all fixed up, except for some odd stains in the upholstery of the backseat that he couldn't get out.

"Things went along okay for a couple of years, but then Cindi started getting restless. She was bored. She wanted to have some fun, and his idea of fun was to watch a game show on TV and go to bed at 8:30. She started drinking again, on the sly. And then one day he came home and her car was gone, and her closet was cleaned out, and there was a note on his pillow saying that she needed some space and was going away for a while.

"Bob was pretty good about it. She'd show up from time to time asking him to cash a check, and he always gave her the cash, and never tried to deposit the check, which he knew would probably bounce. And her Visa bill came to the house every month and he always paid it. She was working as a dispatcher at a fertilizer plant down near Fresno, and back to drinking hard and partying hard, I imagine. I ran into her one day at a Burger King in Stockton. At first I wasn't sure it was her. She looked twenty years older. But it was, and we had a little conversation, and I told her I'd tell Bob I'd seen her, and she said, 'Please don't.'

"Cindi got in a car wreck, totaled the Trans Am, and got pretty scratched up herself. She came home and Bob took care of her, and bought her a new car. It was an '84 Buick that had belonged to an old lady at the church. A real dorky car, but a lot quieter and more comfortable than the Trans Am, and Cindi got to where she liked it well enough. After six weeks she went back to Fresno."

"Do you think they'll get back together again?" I asked.

"Beats me," said Doug. "She may finally get the wildness out of her and be ready to settle down one day."

The soccer game ended, Blue Dolphins winning two to one. I told Doug I'd remember him to Bob next time I saw him.

It was a couple of months later; I'd finished my fall planting and had a flat and a half of broccoli seedlings left over. I called Bob to see if he wanted them. He said he did. I had an errand to run in Vacaville; I told him I'd drop them off on the way.

Bob and Sparky and I took a walk around the place and talked about the weather, and markets, and crops. He invited me in for a cup of coffee. His kitchen looked as if it had been remodeled in 1951 and not touched since; linoleum counters, cupboard doors with heavy enamel paint. On the wall was a framed photograph of Bob as a younger man, standing with his arm around a woman with curly hair and sultry eyes. She had a seductive look on her face. He had a look on his face, too: clueless, but happy.

"That's my wedding picture," said Bob. "My wife's a career woman. Has a job down in the San Joaquin Valley. So it's one of those commuter marriages. We're hoping she'll be able to retire one of these days and move back up here."

"That would be good," I said. "It's hard being apart." And as I said it, I felt a little flash of annoyance with myself for having underestimated Bob's character. He was steadfast to the core.

Frank and Lisa Ricci

FRANK AND LISA RICCI lived on a farm way out in the sticks, in
Colusa County. To get there from my place, I would first drive north
for an hour on the interstate, then exit onto a two-lane paved road
for about fifteen miles, and then branch off onto a one-lane gravel
road that heads northward into the Colusa basin, a partially drained
swamp where the principal crop is rice and the principal livestock is
mosquitoes. The Riccis' place was at the end of that road.

The farm had been in Frank's family since gold rush days. There
was a crooked old house built about 1860; the walls were just red-
wood one-by-twelves running vertically nailed to similar boards
running horizontally, and plastered on the inside. There were no
studs, and there was no insulation. There were several old barns
jammed full of stuff, and a miscellany of other little buildings and
sheds. Eight months out of the year, the north wind howled and
made desolate sounds in the telegraph wires. The other four
months, it was hot and muggy. In the hot season you could stick a
tin cup out the window and wave it back and forth a few times and
fill it with mosquitoes; if your recipe called for that ingredient, it
would be no trouble at all to procure it.

The Riccis grew flowers, mostly for drying, although in summer
Frank went to a farmers' market in Lake County, a place even more
poverty-ridden than Colusa County. Their main business was selling dried flowers over the Internet; when they wanted the UPS man
to pick up a shipment, they posted a flag down at the paved road.

They had a big vegetable garden and some fruit trees, and they kept chickens, and that supplied most of their food. The Riccis worked hard, but not particularly effectively, and their income was pitiful. But there was no mortgage on the place; they had only to pay the property tax and electric bill. They heated the house with an old iron stove by burning orchard prunings, and they cooked on the same stove. Water was heated in a massive copper cylinder with a little firebox on the bottom—the finest technology of 1880. There was no need for propane, and hardly any need for electricity. The Riccis were nearly independent of the energy industry, not because of proudly held principles, but simply because that industry never reached their place and they never sought it out.

The nearest school was an hour's drive and not worth the trip, and so their two boys were home-schooled. I thought it would be lonely for them out there in the middle of nowhere with no play-mates, but that wasn't the case. They were connected to a vast net-work of home-schooled kids in remote places by means of the Internet, and their social and intellectual lives took place on that fifteen-inch fluorescent screen. The boys were very articulate. Perhaps it's because the usual collateral modes of communication—facial expression, gesture, tone of voice, a hand on the shoulder—were denied to them. Their only tool was language, and so they became adept at it.

One time when I was out at Frank and Lisa's, I asked Frank what was in the barns, for I'm always curious about the contents of old barns. Frank got a key and opened the biggest barn. As my eyes grew accustomed to the dim light, I began to make out what was there. There must have been twenty-five old cars and trucks parked every which way; a few Model T's, as one would expect, but also some surprises—a Graham-Paige in beautiful shape, an enormous thirties Packard with running boards and dual side-mount spares, a handsome little Studebaker pickup truck. Old two-cylinder John Deere tractors were angled here and there in the gridlock. There was old horse-drawn stuff, too, buggies and wagons, and piles of buggy wheels. All of it was covered with dust and festooned with cobwebs. In one corner I came across an ornate cast-iron stove, and an old Victrola, and shelves of ceramic crocks with lids. On top of every surface, including the cars, there were barrels and boxes and baskets of stuff—dishes and souvenirs and antique ladies' hats and magazines and cancelled checks from the 1920s and 78 rpm records. I picked up a few records and looked at the labels: Bob Wills and the Texas Playboys, Art Tatum, Louis Armstrong. An old forge stood in one corner of the barn, hundreds of blacksmith tools hanging from overhead. There was a woodworking area with a collection of wood-bodied planes and dozens of old handsaws. Another little niche stashed full of tools puzzled me; Frank explained that those were leatherworking tools from the days when manufacturing and repairing harnesses and saddles were a regular part of farm work. A shelf held old handblown jars of seedy glass in which some now unrecognizable vegetable had been put up eighty years ago. Some of the jars still had liquid—others just shriveled little mummies.

Later that evening, Frank was lamenting the high cost of medication for the younger boy, who has a chronic disease, and how tough the family budget had become on account of this. "Maybe you should consider selling some of that stuff in the barn," I said. "You've got half a million dollars' worth of antiques out there."

"No," said Frank. "That's old family stuff. We wouldn't sell it." The way he said it, I knew that it was not negotiable. Too bad. There were some things in that barn I would readily have bought for myself. Mentally I was already rebuilding the carburetor on that Studebaker truck.

In a way, I could see his point. His family had been in that bleak place for probably six generations, and nothing had been thrown out. There was a cumulative sense of family history in that barn, the Packard from a brief period of prosperity, canning jars from an era of frugality. Frank's boys could pick up a hammer that had been used by their great-great-grandfather and pound a few nails with it, and the feel of that wooden handle in their hands gave them a connection to the past that most kids have no inkling of. I wondered what Frank and Lisa's contribution would be to the family's material history. Frank's Ford truck seemed overdue to join its kin in the barn, but other than that, they hadn't bought much of anything in their lives. Their monthly purchases amounted to a pound of salt and a bag of flour and a few cans of coffee. Perhaps the computer would one day wind up in the back seat of the Packard, another little increment of history.

In grade school we are taught to admire people who change the world—Eli Whitney and Thomas Edison and the Wright brothers. We are taught this because it is to the benefit of the ruling powers of society to have such people around. But to some of us it is obvious that the world has changed in the last few hundred years for the worse rather than the better, and that those champions of change might better be reckoned culprits than heroes. Surely the airplane is the worst invention of human history, having driven God from heaven with His hands over His ears. He's hardly been seen since. For whatever reasons, and I don't know what they are, Frank and Lisa have accepted their world as they found it, and have not sought to change it; they will not leave much of a trace. I admire that. I would rather keep the company of such people than those who are impatient for a brave new world.

Couples

AFTER A FEW BLUNDERS, I have learned not to make any assumptions about couples that I see in the marketplace. A fifty-year-old man with a twenty-year-old woman? It could be his daughter, it could be his girlfriend, it could be his wife. A fifty-year-old woman pushing a stroller with a baby—is she the mother or the grandmother? Is that baby a boy or a girl? I don't go there, though I have found that it is always safe to say, "What a baby! Such an intelligent face!" If my customer is a youngish forty-something woman with what is obviously her college-age daughter, it's okay to ask, "Are you sisters?"

Javier, the egg man, takes the opposite approach. When he sees an older man with a younger woman, he makes a point of referring to her as his daughter, even if it's obvious that they're mismatched lovers. It's his way of expressing disapproval.

In general, there is parity in attractiveness among couples: a handsome man and a beautiful woman, or a funny-looking man with a funny-looking woman, or an obese man with an obese woman. Sometimes the two appear to be supermodels—each the other's fashion accessory. When I see a repulsive man with a handsome woman, then I look around for the Rolex watch and the handmade shoes and the clumps of diamonds, for men can use money to purchase rank in this game, just as British aristocrats used to purchase commissions as high-level officers in the army.

Mike Madison

There was a man I had seen at the farmers' market for years—forty years old, more or less, with lumpy, unattractive features, and a prominent Adam's apple, and a bad haircut. He would stand in one spot for fifteen or twenty minutes, staring into the distance. Then he would move a few paces and look the other way, again staring into the distance, his eyes focused a few hundred yards off. One time I crept up behind him and looked over his shoulder to see what it was he was looking at, but I couldn't make out anything exceptional. He seemed a lost soul.

I had a customer who bought flowers from me, a woman, maybe forty years old, prematurely gray. She was nervous and indecisive, with a jittery and unpredictable way of moving. She couldn't reach for a bouquet without damaging half a dozen others around it. She would start a sentence but abandon it halfway through and start another, so that her conversation was all fragments. Half the time I had no idea what she was talking about.

One night at market I looked up and saw the two of them, the man with the faraway look and the jittery woman, walking hand in hand. She was not jittery; she seemed calm. And he had reeled in his gaze from the distance and was looking just at her. They wore matching, irrepressible smiles.

Jeepers, Creepers

THE HUMAN MIND IS A CURIOUS THING. When we are thinking formally, our thoughts seem to proceed deliberately, if not majestically, along a straight avenue, with vistas left and right down intersecting mental boulevards, in a way that would have made Descartes happy. But this is a small minority of the time. More often our thoughts scamper across the rooftops, slide down a drain pipe, duck in an open window, emerge moments later from a distant doorway wearing an odd hat, and disappear round a corner down an alley. Occasionally we get a glimpse of this mental pathway, too.

I often sing while I'm doing farm work. I sing ballads and hymns, blues and Beethoven quartets—all four parts. No doubt a mockingbird in a bush would have a low opinion of the whistles and grunts that represent the perfect music I hear in my head. One day I was harvesting tulips for market—about a hundred and fifty dozen, so it was taking most of the morning—and I noticed that I was singing a song that I had not thought of in at least fifteen years. It was a silly tune, with the lyrics "Jeepers, creepers, where'd you get those peepers? Gosh all get out, where'd you get those eyes?"

Where had this tune been for those fifteen years? And what brought it to mind at this particular moment? It must have been stored in some musical neuron, waiting endlessly in the wings for its audition. From time to time the neuron would be enlivened by a few stray molecules of caffeine tumbling along a nearby capillary. It might feel vicariously the tenseness of a decisive moment, or be lulled by some passing essence of cabernet. But mostly it mutely waited. And then, one day, after fifteen years, the call came: "You're on!" The neuron sprang to life, clicked its heels, and danced out into the spotlight of consciousness to deliver its lines: "Jeepers, creepers, where'd you get those peepers? Gosh all get out, where'd you get those eyes?"

As I thought about this, and wondered what other musical fragments I had stashed away, I realized what the cue had been. It was the name of the tulip I was harvesting: "Mrs. John T. Scheepers," an elegant, yellow, late-season tulip. It does not take much of a slur to get from "Scheepers" to "Jeepers"—two martinis should suffice—and there you have it. And now that that elderly neuron has auditioned and got the part, I can no longer pass within fifty feet of the tulips without its bursting into song: "Jeepers, creepers..." If I had planted some other yellow tulip, Golden Appeldoorn, or West Point, that neuron might have had to wait another fifteen years, or perhaps it would never have been called at all.

Jimmy Jessup

I HAD SEEN JIMMY JESSUP A NUMBER OF TIMES before I met him. I would be driving down a backcountry road and I would spy him walking along the roadside or cutting across a pasture, a disheveled, wild, middle-aged man with a big belly, being pulled along by a little dog straining on a length of rope.

I roam about on foot a good deal myself, and eventually I did run into him. I introduced myself and extended my hand, but shaking hands was not something Jimmy did. As I got to know him, I realized that probably he went for a year or more at a time without touching another human being.

There was something screwy about Jimmy's eyes. When he talked with you, one eye would stare at your left knee and the other would be looking over your right shoulder. When he spoke, he stammered. He must have been teased mercilessly in school. Probably by the time he was in junior high school he begged to be allowed to stay home and avoid that torment, and his mother indulged him, and so he had grown up without socialization. The give-and-take of dialogue eluded him entirely; his conversation consisted of fragments of monologue connected by a mysterious thread known only to him.

I ran into Jimmy from time to time and always stopped to say hello. When he got used to the idea that I would listen to what he had to say and not ridicule him, and when he was finally reassured that I wasn't going to try to convert him into a Jehovah's Witness or sell him aluminum siding, he relaxed a bit, and over the course of a couple of years I got a picture of his history and his situation.

Jimmy's grandparents had farmed forty acres of citrus in the Los Angeles basin starting in the 1920s. By 1953 their grove was surrounded by housing on all sides, and they gave in to pressure and sold to a developer. The proceeds sufficed to buy twelve hundred acres of good land in my district. When the old folks died, the land was split three ways, and some of it was sold off, and some was traded. When Jimmy's parents died, they left Jimmy and his sister joint ownership of just over three hundred acres, two-thirds of it in walnuts and the rest in row crops.

Labor on the farm was done by a few Mexicans who knew what to do without much in the way of instructions. Jimmy's main responsibility was to mail in the property tax once a year and keep the utilities paid up. There was no mortgage on the place, and Jimmy took home about eighty thousand dollars in a good year, and about fifty thousand in a poor year. Like many people whose wealth is unearned, he was a rabid Republican. He thought that Ronald Reagan and George Bush were far too liberal.

As near as I could make out, Jimmy had no human friends. His dog, confusingly also named Jimmy, was his constant companion. They went everywhere together, and the two Jimmies slept on the same couch. If Jimmy the man would lead his life without ever experiencing a passionate kiss, he at least got his face licked by Jimmy the dog once in a while, which is a sort of substitute. Jimmy had enough money to go to San Francisco once a month, check into a hotel, and have luscious call girls sent to his room (in his situation it's what I might have done), but I don't think he did that. I don't know what he did with his money.

After Jimmy's mother died, he continued living in her house, a low, 1950s ranch house. His housekeeping practices were about what you might expect of a half-wild bachelor. He lived on chili con carne straight from the can, unheated, and peanut butter sandwiches, and oranges from a few dooryard trees when they were in season, which was about seven months of the year. His only drink was water. Once a year or so he cleaned the house—he threw the empty cans into the garage. He washed his clothes by going fully dressed into the former swimming pool, now converted to a pond replete with water lilies and fish and ducks. When he came back out, he emptied the pollywogs from his pockets and walked around until the clothing dried. In the cold season he skipped laundry for a few months.

What Jimmy lacked in human contact, he made up for with the companionship of animals. In addition to Jimmy the dog, he had a couple of dozen cats, and exotic pigeons, and snakes, and an iguana. He had built owl boxes around his place and at dusk would stand in the barnyard conversing with the owls, or so it seemed to him. His great passion was bats. Years before, someone had given him instructions for building a bat house and he had built one, and within a month, bats were living in it. Encouraged by this, he built dozens more and hung them throughout the orchard land. If he found an injured bat, he brought it into his house and cared for it, with no thought for the possibility that the animal was rabid. He would climb a ladder and open the bat houses to check on the inhabitants, petting them with his fat fingers, and murmuring to them in what might have been their own language.

In every culture there are individuals who are cast out of society and live on its fringe. Marked at birth by some oddity—a colored splotch on the face, or crossed eyes, or a stutter—they are teased and cursed and driven from human company. They become witches and sorcerers, despised and also feared. Often, they have a special relationship to animals, and can speak animal languages. Jimmy fit into that tradition, and indeed, his choice of a bat as his totem was a very traditional one. The bat is a good and helpful animal that is ugly and nocturnal and misunderstood, and therefore despised, and Jimmy's affiliation with bats was laden with obvious symbolism.

In Jimmy's case, there was an interesting twist to this old, old story. For Jimmy began to change his farming practices to benefit the bats. He was concerned that the bats might not have enough to eat over the winter, so instead of leaving the orchard floor plowed bare, or spraying it with herbicides, he planted bell beans and clover and mustard to attract and breed insects for the bats to eat. The bell beans and clovers and vetches fix nitrogen and enrich the soil, and they grew so abundantly that Jimmy was able to stop buying and spreading chemical fertilizers. The bats became so numerous that they completely wiped out the coddling moth and navel orange worm, the two principal pests of walnuts; Jimmy was able to give up the practice of spraying insecticides. On behalf of the bats, Jimmy developed hedgerows and meadows and little vernal ponds around the perimeter of his place; these attracted birds and snakes and abundant insect life. By an unorthodox route and unorthodox motivation, Jimmy had become an organic farmer. If you called him this, he would have been deeply offended, for he regarded organic farmers as radicals and subversives, even worse than Democrats. And yet his farming practices were such that if he had applied for organic certification, it would have been granted.

Listening to Lilac

THERE IS A SWALE ON MY PLACE where cold air collects, and where lilac bushes grow happily. In April I take cut flowering branches of lilac to the farmers' market.

I unload my van at the market, setting out on the ground my buckets of lilac, buckets of irises, buckets of ranunculus, some late tulips, a few late anemones yet. By sunrise the early customers are striding through the market. Here comes one now, fiftyish, gray pixie haircut, glasses, basket under the arm, purposeful stride. As she passes my stand, she looks over, then stops. "Lilacs!" It is at once a question, an answer, an exclamation. She approaches my stand, picks up a bunch of lilac, holds it to her face, closes her eyes, inhales deeply, holds her breath for a count of three, exhales, and then begins to talk.

"The spring I was seven years old, my mother was in the hospital. I went to live with my grandmother on her farm in Illinois. Outside the back door of the house was an enormous lilac bush, with a hollow space under it like a cave. My cousin and I spent hours sitting under that bush, talking and catching bees."

"Were you ever stung?"

"No."

"Those must have been gentle bees, or maybe you were gentle children. Would you like a bunch of lilac? They're four dollars."

"Do they last?"

"Not too well. They're undependable. Maybe three days. Cut the stems into hot water when you get them home."

"Yes, I'll take a bunch."

The reaction to lilacs is so stereotypical that a sociologist looking over my shoulder would have it fully described in less than an hour. The glance; the recognition; eyebrows raised, posture frozen; the exclamation; the approach; the scooping up of a bunch and holding it to the face; the deep inhale, eyes closed; the holding of breath for the count of three; the exhale; and then the monologue. Memories, of decades past and places far off, spoken in a tone almost confessional, the bustle of the marketplace overpowered by the recollection of some other lilac-laden time.

Rumpled academic type, tweed jacket with leather elbow patches, long curls of gray hair stylishly hanging over his collar. "Lilacs!" Eyebrows raised dramatically. Picks up a bunch. Deep inhale, eyes closed, count of three. Drops them back into the bucket. "When lilacs last in the dooryard bloom'd..." he begins, and makes an expansive gesture to encompass the row of etceteras needed to finish the quote. I help him out. "And the great star early droop'd in the western sky in the night, I mourn'd, and yet shall mourn with ever-returning spring." This is the main variant of the monologues of reminiscence—the first line of Whitman's poem. I hear it a dozen times in the course of the morning. It is a rare bird who gets past the first line, however. The memorizing and reciting of poetry is not what it was a hundred years ago.

Chinese lady, about seventy, wheeling a bicycle through the market. "Lilacs!" She parks her bike awkwardly in the middle of the crowd, walks to my stand, picks up a bunch of lilac, inhales, eyes closed, count of three, exhales. "During the war it was not safe to be in Shanghai. My parents sent me to boarding school in England. We wore uniforms—a blazer and necktie. I had such a hard time with the necktie, it would make me cry; sometimes the front part was too long, sometimes it was too short. Life was not easy." As an afterthought she adds, "During the war."

Paunchy businessman, gray hair, bald spot, reading glasses in his shirt pocket attached to a cord around his neck. "Are these lilacs?!" The deep inhale, the eyes closed, count of three, exhale, eyes still closed. "Wellesley, Massachusetts, May of '67, Theresa. Sweet Theresa of the short, short skirts." He inhales greedily.

"She sounds delightful. Would you like to buy a bunch? They're four bucks."

"Yes, yes, good idea." He hums happily while I wrap his flowers in newspaper.

An old lady, eighty-five at least, stepping carefully through the market, hair white, dark green beret askew, transfixed by a silver pin, green overcoat, eyes of Ming dynasty blue-and-white porcelain. "Lilacs!" She picks up a bunch of lilac, holds it to her face, inhales, eyes closed. Molecules of lilac scent tumble upward in the air stream, alight in her nasal passages, find the chemoreceptors on nerve endings into which they fit like a key into a lock. Antique neural circuits hum to life. I wait expectantly.

"When lilacs last in the dooryard bloom'd, and the great star early droop'd in the western sky in the night, I mourn'd, and yet shall mourn with ever-returning spring. Ever-returning spring, trinity sure to me you bring, Lilac blooming perennial and drooping star in the west, and thought of him I love..." By the time she begins the third stanza in her quavering voice, eyes closed, clutching her stem of lilac like a martyr her crucifix, I realize that she knows it all, the whole poem, and will recite it all. The clatter and swirl of the market-place fall away. We are enclosed in an intimate bubble, transcending the petty linearity of time, together, just the four of us: the dusty farmer with his buckets of flowers; the porcelain-eyed narrator with her stem of lilac; the mournful, whiskery Whitman; and the assassinated Lincoln, supine in his coffin.

Ulf

ULF'S FARM WAS A STUDY IN GREEN. There was the lime green of Bibb lettuce and the arctic green of collards and the blackish green of Tuscan kale and the bronze green of mustards and the variegated green of cilantro, and many other shades of green, all set out in long, straight rows. The glowing pointillist dots of chiles and tomatoes and oranges were missing, for Ulf did not grow these things. He was a leaf man. He just grew greens.

Ulf himself dressed in green: a faded green t-shirt, green corduroy trousers, and thick green socks with sandals. I never saw him wear any other footgear than socks and sandals, even when he was driving a tractor. He was in his sixties, slender, clean shaven, with a full head of silver-gray hair pulled back into a ponytail, and eyeglasses with large rectangular frames. Ulf spoke so softly that you had to strain to hear him; his voice had a soft fuzziness to it, like an old wool sweater.

The image that I have in my mind of Ulf is of him kneeling motionless before a flowering plant of kale, peering intently at it. He was studying insect life. He knew all the insects on his farm, their Latin names, all their stages of development, and their habits. He didn't just know all this academically, as a professor might—he seemed to know all the insects personally. He knew the birds and rodents and reptiles and fungi and weeds, too, but insects were his main interest. "I don't consider there to be good bugs and bad bugs," he said. "They are herbivores or carnivores. The herbivores eat my crops, and the carnivores eat the herbivores." His farm office was stuffed with books—floras and monographs and treatises—and he knew the literature well, but he relied mostly on his own observations. "Nature is my mentor," he would say.

Ulf farmed eighty acres of greens, and none of the land was idle. If a piece didn't have a crop on it, then it had a cover crop—clover or fava beans or oats. When Ulf had finished harvesting a bed, he didn't necessarily mow it and plow it down right away, for there might be some beneficial beetle or wasp developing in the bed, and he wanted to wait until that insect had matured and migrated before disturbing it. He had all of this figured out very carefully, and in managing his farm he spent more time on his hands and knees peering at bugs than he did driving a tractor. You might see a farm down the road with big diesel tractors roaring around the place, all sorts of activity going on, and you would think, "This farmer's really on the ball." And then you would come by Ulf's place and see him squatting motionless and silent, staring at a bed of parsley, and you would think, "This farmer's asleep on his feet." And you would be wrong. For Ulf was the most alert farmer in the district—he knew exactly what was happening on his eighty acres. The whole trick to growing greens is to keep the bugs under control, and no one did a better job of this.

In his work Ulf gave the impression of being at leisure, never in a hurry, almost offhanded in his decisions. He instructed his crews in his quiet and unhurried way, and they went about their tasks purposefully but without rushing. But despite its easygoing appearance, Ulf's place was extraordinarily productive and efficient. He had a modern packing shed, and two refrigerated trucks making deliveries five days a week. I never talked money with him, but I expect he must have had quite a bit put away somewhere.

I sometimes make fun of organic farmers. The organic code is not the coherent work of a single, profound individual. It is the product of a bickering committee, and it is full of bitter compromise and startling illogic. A thoughtful farmer would sign his name to it reluctantly. There are some who don't bother to think it through; they parade around wrapped in the organic flag, in love with this identity. Others are shysters who see the word "organic" as an opportunity to double their prices. It is easy to mock them. But Ulf did not fall into those groups, although his place was one of the first to be certified organic. I never heard him preach the organic religion, or even mention the word. I believe that he was so absorbed in the complexity of farming well and nonviolently that he didn't think much about organic politics one way or the other.

If I could choose one farmer to emulate, it would be Ulf. But my personality isn't put together that way, and I'm not able to be like him, which doesn't in any way decrease my admiration. I always think of his name together with an epithet; in my mind he is Ulf, the Zen Master of Collard Greens.

Turnip Man

THERE IS A SHOPPER I SEE IN THE MARKET from time to time. I call him the turnip man. He has a huge, bulbous torso, like a turnip, that tapers down to very tiny feet. He's about six and a half feet tall and weighs maybe three hundred and fifty or even four hundred pounds. The turnip man doesn't buy anything from me, or even notice my stand; he has his four or five vendors that he patronizes. I see him leaving the market, his arms hanging straight down, stretched by the weight of bags bulging with baked goods and fruit, their plastic handles looped through his curled fingers.

There are two surprising things about the turnip man in addition to his size. The first is his age; he must be close to eighty years old. And the other is the expression on his face—an incandescent smile. I suspect that even when he's asleep, or lost in thought, or listening to music, the furrows and creases in his face form themselves into a smile, giving him an expression of radiant happiness and goodwill.

By all rights, a person of his size should be long dead. His survival violates an axiom of physiology, first figured out with studies of rats, but applicable also to other mammals. And that axiom is: The less you eat, the longer you live. In humans this axiom takes the form of the forty-five-million-calorie diet. It works like this. Starting at age fifteen, you have forty-five million calories of food that you can eat, and then, other things being equal, you die. The glutton who packs away three thousand calories a day dies in his fifties. The average eater with his two thousand calories a day makes it into his seventies. And the lean and wiry person who eats frugally lives into his nineties.

The loophole in all this is the phrase "other things being equal." Other things never are equal. And so all sorts of inequities and irregularities are to be expected in the application of the rule. The calorie is not the only currency in this economy. A half a minute of worry, or a quarter minute of anger, is about equal to a calorie, and all these debts are paid out of the same account. The exchange rate is not precise; anger and worry and chocolate truffles trade at fluctuating rates, like the dollar and the euro, but whether the markets are up or down, the balance is always falling. The miser of food, thinking that he is preserving his capital, is as often as not a spendthrift with worry and dies sooner than he should.

I believe that the turnip man has survived by shrewdly trading currencies. He cashed in all his worry and anger, and took the payment in calories. And that is how it came to be that at age eighty, weighing three hundred and fifty or even four hundred pounds, he is still alive, happily shuffling through the market, laden with bags of peaches and grapes, avocados and scones.

Meredith

ONE WEDNESDAY I NOTICED that there was a new farmer at the market, and when business was slow I wandered down to introduce myself. "Meredith's Organic Produce," said the sign. "Are you Meredith?" I asked. She was. She was a sturdy woman, thirty-something I would guess, wearing hiking boots and shorts and a long-sleeved jersey. Her hair was in a braid down her back. She wasn't beautiful in a *Cosmopolitan* cover girl sort of way, but she was handsome as robustly healthy people sometimes are.

Meredith had set out a small display of carrots and beets and radishes, bok choy, lettuce, escarole, green onions, and a few other such things. The root crops were scrubbed clean, and the produce was presented with care and obvious affection. There wasn't much of it, though; it had all fit in a little Honda hatchback. Meredith told me that she had rented an acre of ground, and that this was her first attempt at farming, and her first market, and she was nervous. "Don't worry," I said. "Your produce is beautiful. You'll have no trouble selling it." She told me where her farm was and gave me permission to visit sometime.

It was a few weeks later that I was driving down a country road and noticed someone in a field pulling a grain drill with an old two-cylinder John Deere Lindeman crawler. This is a rare tractor, and I hadn't realized that there was one in the area. I pulled off onto a side road so I could watch the tractor and listen to the distinctive sound of its engine, the way a birder might pull off to watch an unusual heron in a field. As I was preparing to leave, I realized that where I had turned off was the road leading to Meredith's farm. I drove on down to have a look.

I spotted her little Honda and pulled in beside it. Meredith laid off pulling weeds and came to see who was visiting. She remembered who I was and gave me a tour of her farm—more of a garden, really, than a farm. "I double dug all these beds by hand," she said proudly.

"You hand-dug these? You don't have a tractor, or even a rototiller?"

"Well, this land is organic, and I didn't want to use any synthetic chemicals on it, including fossil fuel, even though the organic code allows it. It just didn't seem to be in the right spirit." I was impressed. I've always been skeptical of those organic farmers who are so insufferably self-righteous about not using synthetic chemicals but who drive up and down the place in a tractor spewing carcinogenic diesel smoke all over their crops. I felt like I'd finally met an honest organic farmer. A little bit cuckoo, perhaps, but honest. "Of course," she went on, "my car uses fossil fuel, and the UPS truck, and so on, but I wanted to spare at least this piece of land."

"That's admirable," I said, but at the same time I was thinking to myself, "I bet she's not making even two dollars an hour." She had told me that her husband was a mechanic at the state motor pool; probably he made a good wage and had good benefits. Perhaps her farming was meant as some kind of spiritual practice rather than a business, but I didn't ask.

The following Wednesday, just as the market was beginning, I glanced down the aisle, and there was Meredith with a stricken look on her face. I came out from behind my tables and walked down to her stand. "Is everything okay? You look troubled."

"Oh," she said, "the very first customer bought my most beautiful bunch of carrots and three heads of radicchio, and it's ruined my display. It was so beautiful, before."

"Yeah," I said, "they have a way of doing that, the buggers, buying up the best stuff first." Most of the farmers bring a whole truckload, and only a small part of it is set out for display. As produce is sold, they replace it from their reserves. But Meredith didn't have much produce, and it was all set out, with no backup. Perhaps she had a mental image of herself standing behind her tableau of vegetables, a golden nimbus around her like the gilded rays streaming from a medieval Madonna; and all her labor, whether she was conscious of it or not, was directed toward fulfilling this image. Now, just as she had achieved her dream, the very first customer had come along and handed her a couple of shabby dollars and wrecked it.

I dropped out of the market for the winter in late November; Meredith had quit a few weeks earlier. The following spring I expected to see her back, but she didn't show, and one day when I was in the neighborhood I drove down the little road to her acre. The place was abandoned. Some unharvested bok choy had bolted; its flower stalks waved in the breeze. The ground was coming up in bindweed and thistles.

In May Meredith came through the market and stopped to say hello. "I see you've given up the farming business," I said.

"Yes," she said. Patting her belly, which was getting big, she smiled and said, "I'm growing a different crop now."

"Congratulations!" I said. "That's wonderful." As she walked off, I reflected that maybe her year of babying her little crops of tender vegetables had been not a business at all, but a trial run at motherhood, a great welling up of maternal instinct that now had found its rightful object.

Eric, the Dane

Eric, the Dane, had a characteristic way of telling a story. He always started by saying, "Americans are so stupid." Then he would relate a tale of how he had got the better of someone in a negotiation, or how he had taken advantage of an ambiguity in a rule, or how he had abused a lenient policy. Since he was not a citizen, but a guest in this country, I thought it tactless of him at the very least.

Eric had lived in southern California for a couple of years before moving to our area, and when I first met him he spoke excellent idiomatic American English. His peculiar shoes gave away his foreign origin more than his accent did. But he figured out that Americans are deferential to Europeans, and that we are willing to believe that European things are better than American ones. Is not a Volvo superior to a Chevrolet? And so he began to cultivate a Danish accent, and each year it became stronger, until at times I could hardly understand him. Being Danish became his identity. Though he had been no patriot at home, he flew a Danish flag at his stand at the farmers' market. His sign read, "Fresh Produce, Finest European Varieties," and if he was growing a standard American variety, like an Early Girl tomato, he would give it a bogus French or Italian name and use that as an excuse to double the price.

To the amusement of the rest of us, Eric fell for his own propaganda. With great expense and difficulty he had a Volvo tractor imported through Canada, as they are not sold in this country. "I thought Volvo was Swedish," I said to him.

"Yes, the tractor is made in Sweden, but it's pure Danish design, you see."

As it turned out, the pure Danish-designed Swedish tractor was a lemon, and it broke frequently, and sometimes it took weeks for a part to be sent from Sweden. Eric would rage about the inefficiency of U.S. Customs, as if that were the source of his problems. I was barely able to restrain myself from pointing out to him that if he had bought a John Deere, he could have gotten any part he needed at the dealership a mile down the road.

At first Eric leased land, but in three years he had enough money set aside to buy eighty acres of his own. His farmers' market sales were in cash, and it was easy to hide income from the tax man. (Americans are so stupid.) Eric had attended an agricultural college in Denmark, where he had received a thorough, practical education. Unquestionably he was a better farmer than the rest of us, who had blundered into farming from other professions and figured things out by trial and error. His eighty acres were beautifully cared for. He had enough land to use long cycles of crop rotation without running out of space. The land not in crops was devoted to clover or beans or some other soil-building plants. Chickens and goats were integrated into the recycling and composting program so that no bug-eaten leaf or misshapen vegetable would go to waste. Eric had started with excellent soil, and each year he made it better. His orchard trees were pruned perfectly; they looked like illustrations from a textbook.

The work was done by Mexicans, who were paid minimum wage with no holidays and no benefits. If a worker became restive after a few years without a promotion, he was free to leave. There were others who would be happy to take his place. Eric never learned more than half a dozen words of Spanish, but the crews came to know what was expected of them.

When Eric left Denmark, he left behind an ex-wife and child. In southern California, he had started another family; this also ended in divorce, which coincided with his move to our area. Soon after he came here, he married an attractive local woman, and within a couple of years they had a girl and a boy. They were fine little children, and the four of them made a handsome family. But then Eric left his wife and took up with another woman. I met the fourth wife-to-be one time. She had extraordinary hypnotic eyes, and I sensed that she could put me into a trance just by looking at me. I noticed that she wore contact lenses, and it occurred to me that possibly Eric had thrown away a good wife and family in exchange for two wafers of green plastic.

If I taught agriculture, and if I were to take my students on a field trip to see a well-run farm, I would take them to Eric's place. The things one reads in a textbook about sustainable agriculture often don't work out in real life, but in Eric's case they did. To what extent this was due to skill or due to luck I don't know, but the result was inspiring. And yet there was one aspect of Eric's farm that was dead wrong. All those exploited workers, and discarded wives, and cheated business associates, and overcharged customers had been treated as if they were disposable resources. Throw one away; another will take its place. In sustainable farming, sustaining the land is only part of the story; sustaining the human relationships is another. Eric had only got it half right.

July 11

Clean out chicken coop
Replace bait in olive fly traps
Repair broken irrigation— orchard
Prune fire blight out of the quince trees
Harvest tomatoes for drying
Thirty bunches of sunflowers to the co-op
Spray clementines
Work up beds for planting, east end
Plant out sunflowers
Plant out zinnias
Start late crop of marigolds
Fertilize gerbera
Repair door latch— walk-in cooler
Start late crop of Piel de Sapo melons
Irrigate melon beds
Set gopher traps in the tuberose beds
Order 200 cases of half-liter bottles
      for olive oil
Wedding flowers to be picked up Friday— 4 p.m.
Harvest nectarines for drying
Chevy— smog check, renew registration
Order tulips, iris, lilies
Cut back chrysanthemums

Nuggets of Wisdom

Some flower crops—sunflowers, for example—are easy money. Even the most expensive hybrid sunflower seeds are less than three cents each, and they will reliably produce, in nine weeks after being poked into the ground, a flowering stem than can be sold for sixty cents wholesale or eighty cents—or even a dollar—retail. If, when the plant is about ten inches tall, you pinch out the growing tip, it will delay flowering by ten days, but then each plant will make three or four saleable shoots instead of just one.

Other flower crops, such as lilies, are of doubtful profitability. The bulbs are expensive, and apparently also delicious, though I haven't tried one myself. As soon as you plant them, all sorts of creatures are after them; gophers and ground squirrels gnaw on them from below, raccoons and wood rats attack them from above, and various little worms and beetles bore and nibble wherever they can get at them. And once sprouted, the shoots are fragile and vulnerable, requiring regular staking to protect them from the wind. An unseasonable bit of hot sunshine can scorch the foliage, or even the buds, which show up about six months after planting. The buds are like gradually expanding little green bananas, and you have to wait until they show color to harvest the stems, which is nerve-wracking, because it takes weeks, and then you get a hot day and you turn your back for a moment and not only do they color up, they go right ahead and open, at which point they're too fragile to handle. For all that, they are wonderful flowers, and, at some level, worth the nuisance.

Bruce, who farms down the road from me, is shrewd at business and has figured out which of the flower crops are easy money. He grows sunflowers on a huge scale over a long season, with many plantings in succession, and makes a good income from them. Bruce attended technical college and business college, where he learned how to run a farm and how to count money, and where he acquired several wise sayings, including "Farming is a business," and "You're in business to make money." He is quite fond of these little nuggets of wisdom, and polishes them several times a day. But however irrefutable they might seem, I don't particularly agree with them. I would agree to "Farming is many things, perhaps the least of which is that it is a business," and "You are in business for various reasons, an incidental one being to make money." Living in my hometown, where I am known to many people, I am more concerned with how I fit into my community than with how much money I can make. This attitude permits me to grow astounding, elegant lilies, sometimes at an economic loss: a pleasure that Bruce, tied down by his business college platitudes, will never be able to enjoy.

Another nugget often repeated by Bruce is "The profit comes at the end of the row." This refers to the investments and expenses of farming being so great that the first ninety percent of the harvest goes to cover the costs, and profit is to be found only in the last little bit. And so he instructs his crews to dig every last potato, no matter how small, and to strip every piece of fruit from the trees, leaving not even one for raccoon and field mouse and mockingbird. Even if this is valid economics, it strikes me as ruthless, and possibly unwise.

But if I am unenthusiastic about Bruce's nuggets of wisdom, can I offer anything better? Perhaps. One, of limited domain, sticks with me because it came to me in the course of a vivid personal experience; it's "When you're burning off a brush pile, don't wear a straw hat." Another is to be found in the Old Testament of the Bible, a work in which there is not much commentary on farming, since the ancient Israelites were herders more than farmers. But tucked away in the book of Leviticus, along with prohibitions against eating camels or catfish, and an unexpected grant of permission to eat grasshoppers and beetles, is this curious bit of wisdom: "And when ye reap the harvest of thy land, thou shalt not reap the corners of thy field." There are many possible interpretations of this, beside the purely literal one. To me it suggests a certain attitude toward gathering the earth's bounty, an attitude that might be stated "Let enough be enough." Wise advice, and not just for farmers.

Mrs. W.

Mrs. W., the wife of Dr. W., the orthopedic surgeon, came through the market from time to time. She often stopped at my stand to talk about the flowers I offered for sale, for she was something of a gardener, but she never bought anything. One Wednesday afternoon I saw her coming through the market, stopping to chat with each vendor. After a while she reached my stand, and looked over my wares, and asked idly about some flowers, but seemed not to listen to my answer. Instead, she looked at me intently and said, "Did you know that my husband has left me, after twenty-eight years of marriage?"

"I'm so sorry to hear that," I said.

"He went off with a woman twenty years younger than him."

"How foolish of him," I said. I stood there, trying desperately to think of what to say, but after a moment she turned and walked away. I could see her at the next stand, telling a baffled Mexican farmer that her husband had left her after twenty-eight years of marriage. The farmers' market is the most public place in town, the closest thing we have to an agora. Spreading this news from vendor to vendor perhaps was her way of coming to believe it herself.

From what I knew of her, Mrs. W. had built her adult identity entirely as the wife and ornament of Dr. W. She did the typical things that a rich doctor's wife does; she played tennis and golf and bridge, and shopped, and ate out, and went to jazzercise, and had her nails done, and went to the symphony without ever losing consciousness of her position as the wife of the great doctor. So when Dr. W. decamped, he took both her wealth and her identity with him, and she was lost. I suspect, too, that she had made the error, common but not universal among wealthy people, of believing that her wealth, acquired through no virtue of her own, was a sign of God's special favor. No doubt she expected that when she arrived at the pearly gates, she would be whisked through a VIP entrance instead of having to wait in line like the rest of us.

Mrs. W. is a good-looking woman, green-eyed, with freckles, and I expect that her trade-in value on the open market would net another doctor or lawyer, but one fifteen years her senior, so that she could expect a decade at most of something like her former life, after which she would become a sort of nursemaid. Then again, she might surprise us, and show some inner strength, and take on a career and identity of her own.

A couple of Wednesdays later I again spotted her coming through the market.

She stopped at my stand and remarked on some alstroemeria flowers, and then said, "Did you know that my husband has left me, after twenty-eight years of marriage?"

"Yes," I said, "you told me. Men of a certain age can be such idiots."

"What age is that?" she asked.

"Oh, between about five and eighty, I believe."

She looked at me very closely and asked, "You're not planning on leaving your wife, are you?"

"Not at all," I said. "I'm very happily married," but even as I said it I felt the agenbite of inwit, as if I were telling a lie. It's not that I have any thought of leaving my wife, or committing some infidelity. We are excellently suited to one another, and have a long history, and expect to stay together. I would no more trade in my wife on a new one than I would trade in my tractor. Which is not to say that I don't occasionally admire a new tractor—the curve of its fenders, the tightness of its hitch—but it's purely admiration, not covetousness. My tractor and I have a long history too, and in the course of it we've both lost our shine, and gone a bit loose in the bearings, and begun leaking fluids, but we still get the job done. I expect we'll stay together until one of us dies.

What made me uneasy was not any unconscious thought of infidelity; rather, it was the word "happily," for I'm distrustful of happiness. As I child I was occasionally manic, but mostly quiet and gloomy—in photographs I have the expression of a war orphan—and my congenital gloominess has been intensified by a life of farming. On the farm there are so many forces beyond the farmer's control, and so many things that can go wrong, and so many opportunities for failure, that the farmer's only psychological defense is profound pessimism. If you expect failure, then when a crop fails there is no great disappointment, for it is only what you expected, and if by some chance the crop succeeds, then the pleasure of success is compounded by the element of surprise. The little increments of happiness that fall into my life each day—a letter from an old friend, or a low-flying swallow brushing the brim of my hat as I check irrigation in the orchard—always take me by surprise, and for that are more highly valued.

However frivolous a person Mrs. W. might have been, I never doubted that her unhappiness was genuine, and I have tried, with no success at all, to think of some word or gesture of comfort that I might offer her. My best hope is that the next time I see her at the market, I will be able to tell—even at a distance—by the angle of her spine and the firmness of her stride that she has shed the gilded carapace of her former life and set out to become a new and more worthy person, thereby liberating both of us. At that point, conversation will be easy.

Bruce

BRUCE RUNS AN ORGANIC VEGETABLE OPERATION a few miles from me. His farm is bigger than mine, and busier. Flocks of minimum-wage workers toil in the fields while Bruce is inside, striking deals on the phone or tidying his website. He trucks his fruits and vegetables to San Francisco, where the citizens are accustomed to being fleeced, and he asks outlandish prices with a straight face. In the theater of direct selling, he is a great actor and he has studied every detail. The carefully battered hat, the trace of an English accent, the way he holds a bunch of kale close to himself and makes the customer reach for it, teases her a little, acts as if it is a prized possession with which he is reluctant to part—all these are calculated to give an impression of heightened value. He calls eggplant "aubergine," which he takes as license to charge three dollars a pound instead of a dollar like everyone else.

Perhaps Bruce has noticed that in our society there is almost no relationship between the contribution a person makes and how much he is paid, and under the circumstances, why not stand in the ranks of the overpaid? Picking the pockets of the rich is a fine old tradition. It can seem almost an act of kindness. Many of his customers use price as a surrogate for value. "These three-dollar-a-pound aubergines must be truly exceptional to command such a price," they think, and enjoy and appreciate accordingly.

But I have to wonder: if I could be charging three dollars a pound for eggplant, why do I charge only a dollar? I do not have a good answer to this, except to say that three dollars a pound sounds too high. There's a note of arrogance to it. And it implies a more important position in society than I feel that I have. In the utopia envisioned by B. F. Skinner in *Walden Two,* citizens earned credits in society according to the onerousness of the tasks they peformed. Gardening was awarded hardly any credit, as it was judged to be too pleasurable. I, too, have noticed that the rewards of truck farming are mostly not financial ones. I work at home in comfortable old clothes. No commute, no necktie: that alone is worth ten thousand a year, and defrays a low price on the produce.

Most people do not think of themselves as wealthy. The rheumatologist who is paid two hundred thousand dollars a year looks at the plastic surgeon down the hall who makes four hundred thousand and thinks to himself, "I'm not all that well off, not really rich." And the plastic surgeon looks at the health insurance executive making a million and a half, and thinks the same thing. But I tend to cast my glance downward, at the poor devils toiling in cubicles for a low wage, or slamming together burgers in a fast food joint, or driving a stinking, vibrating truck for endless miles, and I think, "How lucky I am, how incessantly well off." If such a one came to my stand and I was offering eggplant at three dollars a pound, how could I look him in the eye?

Bruce runs his business in cash, and I imagine that he has a satchel full of thousand-dollar bills under his mattress. I do not suppose that this makes his bed any warmer on a winter night, nor makes the sun shine more brightly on his fields than on mine, nor makes a peach taste more sweet. Where Bruce has the clear advantage is in the word: "aubergine," a lovely, musical word, almost a poem unto itself, especially compared to the inharmonious Anglo-Saxonism "eggplant." I believe that I too will take to calling that lustrous black fruit an "aubergine." But I will keep my price at a dollar a pound.

The Miners

"Pity farmers!" said Bob Johnson contemptuously, motioning with his head toward the Miners.

"How's that?" I asked.

"Their whole marketing strategy is based on pity; people buy their produce because they feel sorry for them."

I was surprised to hear such disdain in Bob's voice, when usually he is so mild, but his observation had some truth to it. The Miners' decrepit, unwashed van, a broken window patched with duct tape, a spot of oil spreading on the concrete beneath the transmission, seemed a symbol of weariness and poverty. Their tables, rigged up from old boxes and dog-eared scraps of plywood, bowed dangerously under heaps of broccoli and turnips. A child with tear-stained cheeks and a broken overall strap sat dejectedly on an overturned bucket. The adults were nowhere to be seen. A pitiful tableau—one might well buy their broccoli out of sympathy.

Jack and Sally Miner were not pitiful in themselves, though; they were the pleasantest people you would ever want to meet. When one of them shook your hand and smiled, you could not but believe that they were genuinely happy to see you. And I think that perhaps they were.

In the 1970s, when they were students, Jack and Sally decided to forsake the middle-class suburban lives of their parents and go back to the land. They had no particular experience of agriculture: Sally's degree was in sociology and Jack's was in mathematics. They leased twenty acres of mediocre land an hour's drive from town and jumped into farming with both feet, financing the enterprise with money borrowed (repeatedly) from their families. They bought goats and chickens and geese, and took on some dogs someone wanted to get rid of. They built a house—part underground and earth-covered, part geodesic dome—with various solar features, none of which worked. They did not bother with a building permit, which would have forced them to compromise their independence and to cave in to the conventions of the military-industrial-government complex, and they were far enough down a dirt road that the building inspector never noticed their efforts.

The first years were hard. The goats ate all the crops, and the dogs killed the chickens, and thus the Miners learned about the merits of keeping animals in pens. Jack bought a '36 Chevy truck which soon expired, and various rusting farm implements which were more picturesque than useful. For a hundred dollars he got an old windmill from a neighboring farmstead. They dragged it over to their place, and with fifty or so of their friends pulling on ropes, they tilted the steel tower and mill back into vertical position, and poured a new concrete footing around the legs. There was no well under the windmill in its new position, so it pumped no water; it merely spun, idly and noisily, demonstrating the direction of the wind.

The Miners were very keen on the notion of compost, and they built a splendid compost pile of weeds and straw, chicken litter and vegetable scraps, goat droppings and rotting fruit, to which they added daily. The pile became hot and fragrant; bugs and worms tunneled through it, and threads of fungal mycelium proliferated. On moonlit nights they would lie naked on top of the magnificently fermenting compost, and there, among the egg shells and melon rinds, their five children were conceived—four boys and a girl. Their names were Ché, Humus, Shiva, Gandalf, and Bunny. They didn't bother with doctors or hospitals, and they scorned vaccinations as part of a government-medical-capitalist plot.

The Miners sold their produce at a local independent grocery and at farmers' markets. The quality was so irregular that when they did produce something good, you couldn't be sure that it wasn't by mistake. They felt no shame over their wormy and wilted kale. "It's organic!" they proclaimed happily, figuring that this virtue overpowered any defect. And they had such winning smiles, and such wonderful straight teeth, that for a moment you believed them.

Whenever they saw success, the Miners imitated it. If someone at the market prospered by selling honey, they took up bee-keeping. If another did well with fresh herbs, they tried herbs too. In the end, they did a little of everything: fruit, vegetables, herbs, jam, bakery, flowers, goat cheese, honey, eggs, rabbits, pumpkins. Instead of doing one thing well, they did twenty things haphazardly.

Taking up a rural livelihood was a popular course of action in the 1970s. Some of the Miners' contemporaries decided after a few years that farming was not for them, and gave up the experiment and went back to grad school or took government jobs. Others, who were shrewd and industrious, succeeded at farming. They paid off their mortgages and bought neighboring lands. They had new, reliable equipment, and their skilled crews were well paid. They developed contracts with supermarket chains and pioneered produce sales over the Internet. But the Miners neither succeeded nor gave up. They just kept struggling along. Well-to-do friends lent them money and learned not to expect to be repaid. And when it was time

to buy a new Mercedes or Volvo, kindly people would give the old one to the Miners rather than trade it in, for which the dealer gave you hardly anything anyway.

Jack loved the idea of mechanical work. When he put on his mechanic's hat, tucked a greasy rag in his back pocket, picked up a box of tools, and marched toward a balky vehicle, he was the picture of competence and confidence. But in truth, the more he worked on a vehicle, the worse it ran, and if he stayed with it long enough, he was certain to get it to a state where it would run no more. And so the old Mercedes that had been given to them chugged along for a few months, no one paying any attention to the red light on the dashboard that indicated a shortage of oil, until one day it stopped and refused to go farther. Jack towed it with the tractor over to the barn and began happily dismantling various parts of the engine that seemed like they might be culpable, but he was distracted from his task before finishing it, and the parts got scattered around the farm until there was no hope of reassembling them. At times like this, word would go out that the Miners were out of a vehicle, and then someone would lend them an old Toyota truck or a Chrysler van, never really expecting to see it again.

It seemed as if everyone knew the Miners, and one could not mention the hard plight of the small farmer without someone bringing up their name. Their photogenic faces were to be found on posters and in publications dealing with small farms, Jack posing thoughtfully by his rusting '36 Chevy, Sally standing in a field with a basket of zucchini.

Early on, the Miners discovered that there was a great deal more physical labor to farming than they had imagined. They could not afford to hire help, but they came up with the notion of offering internships. The internship was an educational experience, and therefore no salary was attached to it beyond a place to pitch a tent and all the root crops one cared to eat. The interns were a motley bunch, some drifting, some goofing off for a year before going to law school, some living out romantic dreams of rural life. And so there were always half a dozen miscellaneous young people hanging around the Miners' farm and congregating at their booth at the farmers' market. They seemed to enjoy themselves, and probably worked nearly enough to earn their room and board. After a couple of years, Jack and Sally determined that supervising the interns was time-consuming and tiring. They took on a young couple as minor tenant partners to manage the farm and supervise the interns and take care of the daily chores.

Most farmers I know are solitary sorts, content with the companionship of blackbirds and bees: "Good day, Sir," spoken to a jackrabbit, is enough conversation for one morning. But the Miners seemed always to move in a crowd. If they were going to make apricot jam, they invited thirty people to join them, and jam making became a great, noisy party, and everyone went home with half a dozen quarts, so there was hardly any left to sell. Theirs was surely the most sociable farm in the region; it seemed that everyone had been there at least once.

For years I felt that the Miners' well-intentioned friends, forever helping them with donations of money and vehicles and labor, were doing them a disservice. In keeping the farm afloat, they were depriving the Miners of a fundamental right—the right to fail. To one who is paying attention, failure is a great teacher. I know about this; I've done enough graduate work at the college of failure to have earned several advanced degrees. The Miners were fine people who should not have been farmers; they weren't allowed to find this out.

But I have since come to believe that that analysis is wrong, and that I was missing the whole point. What the Miners were selling was not kale and broccoli and melons and peaches—it was the vicarious experience of an idealized rural life. They were purveyors, or perhaps curators, of an enduring myth. And impending heroic failure is intrinsic to the enterprise, for if the farm were prosperous, its existential edge would be dulled, and its mythic dimension diminished. And so the Miners kept their farm teetering on the brink of ruin, and their urban friends wrote generous checks as a sort of cover charge that let them participate in the fantasy of the little family farm struggling to survive, its righteous and clear-eyed owners keeping up their courage in the face of unfriendly odds. This was nothing so cynical as the Disney-Marriott "Aging Hippie Organic Farm and Petting Zoo," admission $17.50, for it retained its authenticity of purpose. I suppose that the Miners themselves were the most devout believers in the myth. The rusting '36 Chevy and the idly spinning windmill and the goats and chickens and geese and the pack of barefoot children were there for their symbolic value, not their utility. Once you see it, there is an irrefutable logic to them.

In the twenty-first century, operating a little farm for one's livelihood is a rare privilege. Like most privileges, it carries obligations with it. One of these is to share the experience with one's urban friends by talking with them, and writing to them, and inviting them to the farm, handing them a picking basket or putting a hoe in their hands, and letting them work. Whatever we might think of the Miners' ramshackle farming operation, on this point they are far ahead of the rest of us. We could learn from them.

Eat Bitterness

WE DON'T GROW SWEET CORN ON OUR FARM—it takes too much water, and it's a finicky crop, and in the past when we've grown it we've been inattentive and failed to harvest it at the critical moment. So we leave corn-growing to the specialists, and when we want corn we buy it, or barter for it. This year we tried the varieties of sweet corn available at the farmers' market—So Sweet, Milk 'n Honey, Even Sweeter, Candy Store, and Sweet Heart. All of these newer varieties have the sh-2 (supersweet) gene, which causes the kernels to develop an extremely high sugar content. To me they taste too much like candy and not enough like corn. I asked one of the old farmers why he was growing these instead of the classic varieties like Golden Bantam and Trucker's Delight. "Oh, that's what everybody wants nowadays," he said. Not everybody. I guess if I want corn that tastes like corn, I'll have to grow it myself.

The supersweet gene isn't showing up just in corn. There are supersweet varieties of carrots and beets, grapes and apples. When sugar overpowers flavor, it becomes difficult, with your eyes closed, to tell a Red Flame grape from a Fuji apple from a Lutz beet from a Sugar Baby carrot—all of them are crunchy sugar. And as the tools of biotechnology are put to work, we can expect that extra sugar will soon appear in all sorts of unlikely places—peanuts? tomatoes? onions?

I was chatting with the checkout girl in the supermarket one day while she rang up my groceries, and I asked her what was the most popular item in the store. Cap'n Crunch cereal. Sixty percent sugar and crunchy. I wonder if fruit and vegetable breeding isn't sloping downward toward some lowest common denominator of human taste—Cap'n Crunch—instant gratification for a spoiled child.

A traditional Chinese curse translates "Eat bitterness." To a child this is indeed a curse, but to an adult, to eat bitterness is not such a bad destiny. I think of Turkish coffee, escarole, unsweetened chocolate, wild almonds, quinine, winter melon, endives. Bitterness is complex and interesting; it lingers on the palate, and like music in a minor key, it sets a mood of contemplation and regret. The truly terrible curse, which I sometimes suspect is being aimed at all of us, is "Eat sweetness."

Warplanes Overhead,
a Prayer, Romans

Travis Air Force Base lies thirty miles southwest of my
farm, and from time to time a military cargo plane flies over. They
make an odd, whistling sound that sets the coyotes down in the creek
to howling. Today I was walking through the olive grove with a spade
over my shoulder, carrying a bundle of gopher traps, seeking out my
little enemies, when a pair of the big cargo transporters passed overhead at low altitude. They are so huge that it seems implausible that
they can fly. No matter what the position of the sun, the planes cast
a shadow over the whole farm—a shadow that lingers long after they
have gone. The country prepares for war, and Mr. Bush bleats about
the evil Saddam Hussein, all the while planning the deaths of innocent thousands of Iraqis by American bombs.

Our nation is so wealthy and powerful that it can no doubt con-
quer Iraq by bombing it until not so much as a wall is left standing,
so that the oil of that land can be seized without interference, and
our citizens can continue wantonly driving their SUVs. When this
happens, there will be flag-waving and celebrations of victory on
television, but I find in it nothing to be proud of. I do not wish to
be on the winning team. I do not wish to be on any team at all. But
if I must be on a team, let it be a losing one. Let me share the quiet
camaraderie of defeat, and spare me the leaping arrogance of victory.
And if the world must be divided into victors and vanquished, then
let me live in a conquered land, and belong to a despised race. Give
me a remote homestead at the farthest edge of the empire, so far

from the center that the influence of the invaders is attenuated to mere confusion; where the possibilities for subversion are numerous; and where the natives greet one another with a wink, and irony is as rich and abundant as oxygen.

I had only the sketchiest instruction in Roman history in school. And I never read Gibbons' big book, although I once looked at it in the library, admiring the gold lettering on the spine that formed those mighty words—"Decline and Fall." I pulled a volume from the shelf and opened it randomly, feeling the smoothness of the paper and inhaling the scent of the decaying leather binding. The margins were much too stingy, and the type was tiny, in an odd font. I read a few rolling sentences to get a feel for the cadence of it, and then replaced the volume on the shelf. That was my Roman education. If I had thought about it, which I hadn't, I probably would have accepted that the average Roman was a patriot, proud of the expansion of the empire. But I don't believe that now. I expect that the impulse for expansion of the empire came from a little band of profiteers in the capital, together with their minions in the government and the army. Or perhaps it was the governors themselves who were the profiteers, as it is with us, where the oil industry and its mascot in the White House wage private wars of expansion at public expense. The average Roman citizen in the countryside probably grumbled at the burdensome taxes, and worried about the conscription of the young men into the army, and was disheartened by the flood of cheap foreign goods that undermined the local industries. But aside from muttering to himself, he did not protest. So it is that we abdicate our political power to unworthy leaders.

Is Slovenliness Infectious?

SOME PEOPLE, AS THEY GET OLD, become increasingly intolerant. Here is such a one at his breakfast table, reading his morning paper, his face creased into a frown, fuming and muttering. "Damned liberals! Damned gays! Damned whining minorities! Whatever became of all the true Americans? That worthless foreigner at the dry cleaner lost my best shirt. Is there no competence anymore? No good American values?" And so on. Probably he lives in a gated suburban community and drives an enormous SUV with a bumper sticker that says "Buy American," which he looks at proudly while he fills the tank with Arabian gasoline.

Others, as they age, become more tolerant. They recognize that each life has its own interior logic, no matter how fractured it looks from the outside. And they recognize that frailty comes in many forms, and that most people are doing the best they're able with what they have to work with. I find that on the average I am more tolerant than previously, but that there are certain traits—greed, cruelty, wastefulness—of which I am less tolerant. This story is about a little lesson in tolerance.

One morning I awoke with a pain in my side. "It will go away," I thought, and I went about my daily chores. But it did not go away, and it kept me awake most of the night. The next day it was considerably worse. I went 'round to see my doctor. He examined me and said, "You have smoldering appendicitis. Get yourself to the emergency room."

I drove to the teaching hospital in Sacramento and was admitted to the emergency room. They took away my clothes and gave me an undignified garment in exchange, and I was parked on a gurney in a large room full of other gurneys, each with its traumatized or afflicted inhabitant. Medical students came by from time to time to practice their karate moves, jabbing me to see how high I could be made to jump. Various tests were performed, none conclusive. Around midnight a very tired-looking surgical resident examined me. "I think you have a kidney stone," he said. "There's nothing that can be done about it; you might as well go home." So I went home.

Over the next couple of weeks the pain waxed and waned, and I moped around the place, working at half-speed. One night the pain was radically worse, and my wife drove me to the emergency room at the local county hospital, where, as it turned out, my medical insurance was not accepted. A kindly old doctor, Dr. Singh, examined me. "You have appendicitis," he said. "Your appendix is not about to burst, and you won't die tonight, but you need to see a surgeon first thing in the morning and get that taken care of."

The next morning I went to my primary care doc to get a referral to a surgeon. He said, "I can't do that. Your health insurance doesn't work that way. Before we can do that we have to run some tests." He wrote a phone number on a scrap of paper. "Call this number and make an appointment for a CT scan. I'll have an authorization forwarded to them." I called the number. The receptionist said, "We don't have an opening until next January."

"I believe it's somewhat more urgent than that," I said.

"Do you want the January appointment or not?" she asked crossly.

"Okay, I'll take it," I said. Six or eight weeks went by. Some days I was more or less functional, some days I was feverish and depressed. I could feel the painful spot exactly with my finger, and wondered what was going on in there. One night I again was seized with pain, and early the next morning I went to see the on-call doc at my primary care place. He examined me and said, "There's a lump in your abdomen the size of a lemon. You need to get a CT scan right away."

"I've been trying to get one of those," I said. "They're hard to come by." He punched the keys on his telephone and a few hours later I was getting my scan. That night a radiologist telephoned me at home. "I read your scan," he said. "You have a chronic perforated appendix. You need to get that taken care of ASAP. Probably not tonight, but first thing in the morning for sure, you should see a surgeon. I've already sent over your referral, so they'll be expecting you."

The next morning I went to the surgery clinic at the teaching hospital. I was put in a little room and left there for some hours. Finally the surgeon came in, directly from the operating room, dressed in his scrubs and with little paper covers over his shoes. He wore a heavy gold chain around his neck. He said, 'I haven't seen your scan—it's lost in the computer somewhere, but frankly, you don't look very sick to me." Then he turned his back to me and began questioning the students who had come into the room with him about acute abdominal pain in an adult. Could be a carcinoid, could be this, could be that. They ordered a battery of tests for me and sent me home.

Months went by. I was listless and depressed, sometimes in pain, sometimes feverish. A big north wind blew a skylight cover off the tool shed. It landed in the middle of a path. I didn't repair it, I didn't even move it out of the way, I just walked around it. My equipment was overdue for maintenance, and I ignored it. Weeds were growing up in the beds, seedlings that should have been planted out in the field languished in the greenhouse. The place was going to the dogs. We hired a full-time worker to help us, a fine young woman, intelligent and good-natured and strong as an ox. We couldn't afford to pay her what she was worth. I began reading the classified ads in the newspaper, "Help Wanted," looking for some kind of desk job. I felt like my farming career might be about over. But I had no saleable skills. Somehow we made it through the summer and fall. I got some fall planting done—about half the usual amount.

One morning a few days before Christmas, the familiar pain returned in force. My wife drove me to the emergency room at the teaching hospital. By now I knew what to expect—the undignified garment, the gurney in the hall of the afflicted. The medical students were on vacation, so I was spared their attentions. A surgical resident, a bright-eyed young woman, came to examine me. She listened carefully to my complicated history without interrupting me, which I thought was unusual, and very good of her. She examined me and said, "You don't look very sick to me. We'll do a CT scan to rule out the appendix, but assuming that's negative, I think that we should proceed on the assumption that you have an ulcer. We'll scope you through the mouth and have a look."

I passed the day on my gurney, drinking contrast media, and getting my scan, and watching the lively human drama of the ER. Around seven in the evening, twelve hours after I had checked in, the same surgical resident, still on duty, came over to my gurney. She said, "The radiologist has read your scan. His diagnosis is appendicitis. We'll operate as soon as an operating room is available—realistically, tomorrow morning. In the meantime, we'll try to find a room to stash you in."

I was put in a room with three beds. One held a man in a coma who had fallen off a ladder putting Christmas lights on his house and landed on his head. The other patient was strapped into his bed. He shouted all night, in a deep Southern accent. "Untie me, you bitches! Untie me, you bitches! I need a smoke. Roll me outside. Untie me, you bitches!"

The next morning I was wheeled up to the pre-op room. The anesthesiologist said, "I'm going to give you something to make you a little groggy." He put a syringe into the catheter in my arm and began injecting. I felt warmth and sweetness flowing into my arteries. Fifty years' worth of existential knots began to loosen and unravel. The marrow of my bones emitted light. I was washed with forgiveness.

The next thing I knew, I was back in the room with Mr. Untie-me-you-bitches. Across my belly was a row of shiny metal staples. The pain was gone.

Over the next weeks I felt like I was thirty years younger. I arose before dawn, eager for work. I repaired the skylight cover and put it back on the roof. I serviced all my equipment. I pruned trees that were years overdue. I stacked firewood, and graded the roads, and divided old perennial beds. I sat down with my seed catalogues and ordered enough seeds to plant two hundred acres. I was reading the classified ads in the newspaper again, this time "Acreage for Sale," feeling that my little farm didn't offer enough scope for the amount of energy I had. After a few months I did calm down, getting back to the frame of mind I had been in before all this started.

Which brings me around to the question of tolerance. There are some farmers at the farmers' market who are so slovenly it's painful to watch them. They always arrive late, their trucks are unwashed and poorly maintained, and even before their produce is half unloaded they've disappeared somewhere—gone off for a smoke, or a cup of coffee, or a nip from a flask. They seem not to care much about what they're selling, and look like they just wish the market would end so they could get some dinner or go to a tavern and have a drink, or go to sleep. I've always been contemptuous of those farmers. I thought they showed a serious defect of character. But I have to reconsider that opinion, and be more tolerant in my judgment, for I nearly became one of them myself. Maybe they suffer from some abscess, some sequestrum, some pocket of infection that leaks into their bloodstream and poisons their will and undermines their character. Maybe slovenliness is an infectious disease.

Larry

THE ZONING OF FARMLAND IN MY DISTRICT specifies that no parcel shall be smaller than forty acres. The admirable idea behind this is that no family should find itself on a parcel of land too small to make a living by farming it. This spares us the trashy sort of landscape that results when land is divided into little ranchettes of a couple of acres. A lone, bored horse stands in a fenced acre of dust that it shares with five broken-down cars. Off to the side in a clump of ailanthus trees is a pink mobile home, a loose metal panel flapping rhythmically in the wind. A Labrador chews on the tire of an overturned tricycle. The owner is nowhere to be seen; he's half a continent away, barreling down the interstate in his eighteen-wheeler, seriously overdosed on country and western music.

As I say, we're spared that scene, and instead have a handsome landscape of prosperous and orderly working farms. There are a few small parcels here and there that existed before the present zoning laws came into effect, and these are much sought after by urban people who wish to live in the midst of beautiful farm country without paying for the privilege by actually farming. One of these little two-acre places is about a mile from me. It's owned by an older, childless couple: Jeannine is a retired librarian, and Larry is a retired high school English teacher. You might imagine a house full of books and cats, the old folks wearing cardigans and half-glasses, sitting on overstuffed chairs, reading and humming absentmindedly along with the Mozart on the radio. You'd be wrong. Jeannine, who is a youngish fifty-something, has her hair cropped short and dyes it startling colors. She wears a lime green jumpsuit and cowboy boots, and rides a yellow Kawasaki racing motorcycle. I'll be driving down a country road, studying my neighbors' crops, and I'll hear the crescendo of her machine as it rapidly overtakes me. She shoots past in a flash of color, gravel spraying in every direction, and is quickly gone. It's the kind of motorcycle upon which the driver doesn't sit upright, but more or less lies down, with the engine clasped between her knees. I assume that there's some erotic dimension to Jeannine's motorcycling, but I don't know her well enough to joke with her about it. And I could be wrong. It might just be the natural reaction to thirty years of working in a library, whispering and shushing and being unbearably restrained.

Larry stays home and tends a little orchard of about a hundred peach trees. The variety is Fay Elberta, which is nearly the same as Elberta, but it ripens three weeks later. They're big, golden, luscious peaches so juicy that after you eat one you have to take a shower. A competent orchard man, in the course of a year, might spend a total of five days on those trees taking care of pruning, fertilizing, spraying, mowing, thinning the fruit, and propping up overloaded branches. Larry stretches this out to about two hundred and fifty days, making it into a full-time job. His tools are a gasoline-powered weed eater, a chain saw, and a radio the size of a suitcase. He plays appalling music, and he plays it loud. It's not even precisely music, just violent shards of tortured sound. A sensitive person, tied to a chair and made to listen to it, would sign any confession put before him, and would pray for a swift and merciful death. It seems to me that Larry's choice of noise is a sign of severe neurological pathology. But I might be wrong. It might just be the natural reaction to thirty years of trying to teach *The Mayor of Casterbridge* to sullen and hostile adolescents.

A skilled tree man will walk up to a peach tree, study it for a moment, and then make three or four bold cuts with a handsaw, dropping good-sized branches to the ground. He picks up his loppers and makes a few adjustments, and in three minutes he's done. The tree is perfect. He makes it look easy, in the way that any virtuoso performance looks easy. Larry, on the other hand, spends a day or more on each tree. He stands there, with his music blasting and his chain saw idling, studying some minor twig, agonizing over where to cut it. When finally he's done, the tree is hacked and nibbled and chewed, looking as if it has been attacked by rodents. Satisfied at last with his work, Larry advances to the next tree, studying how best to disfigure it.

Larry's place is far enough away from mine that the radio and chain saw are not seriously obnoxious to me, just annoying, like a mosquito in your tent. But one morning, when I had been drinking too much wine the night before and was feeling less tolerant than usual, I decided to have a word with him. I walked over to Larry's orchard, where he was torturing the trees, and called out to him. He couldn't hear me over the noise, and I had to walk around until I was in his field of view to get his attention. When he saw me he shut off the chain saw and the radio. We chatted for a bit, and then I said, "Have you noticed how the orchard guys around here don't use chain saws? They just use a sharp handsaw on an eight-foot fiberglass pole, and a pair of loppers. It's very efficient, and quiet, too."

"I prefer a chain saw," said Larry.

"Well, it's pretty damn loud," I said. "When the wind it is out of the south, I can hear it inside my house, and I don't much care for it. I don't care for the radio, either."

"Is that so?" said Larry. "I thought the chain saw and the radio kind of cancelled each other out."

"Look," I said. "If a bunch of people were in church on a Sunday morning, having a religious service, would you go into the church with your radio and chain saw and fire them up?"

"No, of course not," said Larry.

"Well," I said, "there are people living among us, more than you might think, for whom every moment of every day is a time of worship, and for whom every square foot of the earth is sacred ground, and for whom every increment of the sky is the house of God, and for those people, you're making an appalling racket during a religious service."

"Those people," said Larry, yanking the cord of his chain saw so that it screamed to life with a puff of blue smoke, "are nuts."

Fathers

FATHER AND SON, FATHER AND DAUGHTER: difficult relationships, fraught with cross-purpose. And yet, so often when I see fathers with their children in the market, there is a sweet tenderness there. It is surprising to see in men who, in their professional lives, are ruthless and unforgiving—loan sharks, tax auditors, art critics—men who, if it suited their purpose, would, without scruple, disembowel you. Here's one now—some hatchet-faced lawyer, a Doberman in a suit, patiently teaching his little daughter how to eat a fresh fig. And here comes another—big burly brute, probably has an extra chromosome or two, the sleeves torn off his t-shirt to reveal a cascade of violent tattoos, a man you would cross the street to avoid, and in his arms he carries an infant as tenderly as if it were a soufflé. And the little guy reclines in those huge hairy arms perfectly at ease, non-chalant and insouciant. Amazing.

For most of history, and for probably all of prehistory, we lived in conditions of scarcity—not enough food, not enough caves, not enough women, not enough of anything. And so men became aggressive and pushy and annoying, trying to supply the needs of their families. These traits—partly cultural, partly genetic—were obnoxious but effective, and came to define the predominant persona of successful males.

For the last half-century we have lived not with scarcity, but with abundance. Curiously, hardly anyone seems to have noticed. Male behavior is as it has always been, and men go on slaying their enemies in the workplace quite unnecessarily, merely out of habit.

But in the farmers' market, the myth of scarcity can no longer be maintained. Avalanches of produce on every side shout abundance. There is enough, enough of everything, and it is inexpensive and easy to get. You don't have to fight for it, you don't have to push anyone out of the way. There is plenty. And overpowered by the message from the heaps of produce, these tough guys relax their stance of aggression, and there, with their children, they are finally at ease, generous and forgiving.

Javier, the Egg Man

IN THE SUMMER MONTHS, Javier, the egg man, shaved his head so that it was as smooth as an egg, but he did not shave his thick, black Zapatista mustache. He wore a straw hat, and a freshly ironed white shirt, and bib overalls, and lizard-skin cowboy boots with silver toes. He brought eggs to market in flats of three dozen, which he stacked perilously high on a card table.

Javier had grown up on a ne'er-do-well goat ranch in Texas, and when he was ten years old, his father gave him a fighting chicken. That rooster won twenty fights in a row and retired undefeated, and the young Javier took to breeding him and selling the fertilized eggs at fifty dollars per dozen to men who wanted to take them back to their homes in Mexico. Despite his success with the fighting chicken, Javier recognized that ranching was no way to make a living, and when the time came, he went to college and majored in accounting and became an auditor for the Internal Revenue Service. He ran his egg business on the side because he enjoyed it, and because it put a little unaccounted money in his pocket, and because he wanted his children to have some notion of their family's history.

Javier kept about nine hundred chickens. At night they roosted in a barn, and by day they were turned out to range in a yard. There were four yards of about two acres each. Three of the yards were growing greens, while the chickens were ranged in the fourth. After a few weeks, the birds would have demolished the greens in one yard, and they would be moved to another. The yard just vacated would be disked and harrowed and sowed with seed and irrigated. The seed was a mix of oats and amaranth and lettuce. Javier bought lettuce seed that had passed its expiration date for about five cents on the dollar from a wholesale seed place. When chickens have plenty of greens to eat, the yolks of their eggs are deeply colored, almost the color of a ripe orange, and this was one of the selling points of Javier's eggs at the market.

The standard chicken of the egg industry is the White Leghorn, a prolific producer of eggs but otherwise a miserable sort of bird, stupid even by chicken standards. If you walk up to a group of Leghorns and clap your hands once, they squawk and flap and run hysterically in circles. If you do the same to a group of Rhode Island Reds, they cock their head to one side and study you, as if to say, "What's this joker up to?" Javier had started out with about a dozen breeds of hens—Rhode Island Red, Black Ancona, Silver Spangled Hamburg, Barred Plymouth Rock, Black Minorca, Buff Cochin, Araucana. There were no White Leghorns. For roosters he kept only Araucanas. When he incubated eggs and hatched out the chicks, he would grow the roosters out for twenty-four weeks, and then sell all of them except the Araucanas to a Chinese butcher in San Francisco who was happy to take all he could get. The Araucana roosters were kept for breeding. Over the course of a few years, the identities of the breeds had mostly disappeared into a swarm of hybrids.

I was curious about Javier's breeding program, and asked him about it. He admitted right off that he had no knowledge of genetics. Partly he was simply trying to recreate the type of flock that he remembered from his childhood in the Texas borderlands, where every chicken was an individual, the sole representative of a unique breed. "Those chickens never got sick," he said. "I'm sure it was because they had plenty of space to range around, and clean water, but I think it was also because they were all different. I believe that's healthier. I haven't had any disease problems at all with my birds. But the other thing I've been interested in with my breeding program is the color of eggs. Some of the breeds that I started with lay white eggs, some buff eggs, and some brown eggs. The Araucanas lay pale blue and pale green eggs. By now every egg I get is a different color, and there's just something very attractive about that."

What Javier said was true, and I had noticed that he spent a lot of time at the market repositioning eggs in their flats. He was an artist whose medium was the arrangement of three dozen subtly colored eggs into a grid of six by six. To one who is attentive to color, that afforded sufficient scope for a lifetime of art.

In the twentieth century, the science of agriculture (as opposed to the art of farming) moved in the direction of eliminating diversity. By the end of the century it was common to have a thousand-acre field in which every plant was genetically and physically identical to all the others. The uniformity of the crop simplified the design and operation of harvesting equipment, as well as the industrial processing of agricultural products as they were manufactured into foods and other goods. The move toward uniformity was in opposition to the forty centuries of farming that had gone before, in which the preservation of diversity was considered a virtue. The old Mexican farmer setting aside part of his corn crop for next year's seed makes a point of saving all the variations, for each year is different, and some years one kind will thrive, and other years another kind will thrive. And, as Javier believed about his chickens, a diverse crop of corn is more resistant to disease than a monoculture.

In the twenty-first century, the tools for creating uniformity and eliminating diversity are ever more powerful. And the more powerful the tools one has, the more enormous the blunders one can make, which is how the path of agribusiness looks to many of us. Diversity and complexity are always healthier and more interesting—in chickens, and in corn, and in populations of people, and in ideas.

Old Persian

MANY FOREIGNERS SHOP AT THE MARKET—students from the university, or visiting scholars, or overseas relatives, but their foreignness is of a minor and incidental sort. They are fellow residents of a single global city of which New York and London and Rome and Delhi and Singapore are adjacent neighborhoods, connected by airlines rather than streetcar lines. In their choices of music, and clothing, and automobiles, and amusements, these foreigners hardly differ from the locals.

Occasionally, however, someone shows up at the market whose foreignness is profound and unfathomable. One of these is an old woman of Middle Eastern provenance who dresses in many layers of handmade skirts that reach to the ground, so that just the tips of her Nikes poke out, and who wraps her head in many windings of a voluminous shawl, and who wears dark glasses with huge, opaque lenses. She speaks not a single word of English, not even "hello" or "good-bye" or "thank you." She's always at the market, start to finish, and though she has no money, she gradually accumulates a large bag of produce given to her by farmers with whom she has a nodding acquaintance.

It happened that one day the old Persian woman was shuffling down the aisle while two locals were at my stand looking over tulips that I had for sale. One of the locals said, "Look at that strange old woman," and the other said, "Yes, I've heard about her. She's from Iran and speaks only Farsi. Her son brought her over here to keep house for him, and then he went back to Iran and left her here. Her condominium is paid for, but she has hardly any money to get by on, and she doesn't know a soul here, even after all these years."

The two shook their heads and agreed about what a terrible son he was. I'm not so quick to condemn him. Perhaps the mother was a miserable nag who had a toxic relationship with her daughter-in-law, and the son went back to Iran to save his marriage. Or maybe he just went home on a casual visit and was thrown into prison on trumped-up charges. How can one presume to judge?

It is true that the old woman seems to have no money. But she's proud, and does not accept charity. Instead, she barters; rather, she practices something vaguely like barter. She comes to market with bags of miscellaneous stuff that she's fished out of a dumpster or a trash pile, and she uses it for trading. It's nothing that anybody wants—old vinyl records of obscure singers, or used and somewhat malodorous clothing, or a pink transistor radio that doesn't work. But the farmers accept the pretence of barter, and later, on their way home from market, throw the unwanted trade goods in a trash can.

The old Persian is fond of melons, and when melons are in season, she always comes by my stand to examine them, and pinch them, and smell them. Sometimes, holding up a melon, she delivers a soliloquy in her incomprehensible native tongue. Maybe it's a reminiscence about her homeland—I have no idea. I set aside a few melons for her, and she, in her turn, brings me a canvas jacket of peculiar design with a cigarette hole burned in the sleeve, or a pair of running shorts, size fifty-two.

One afternoon I was picking through my melons, looking for one to set aside for the old Persian, seeking a damaged or inferior one. It's what all the farmers do for her—set aside the bruised peach or the misshapen pepper or the bird-pecked persimmon. As I sorted melons, I got to thinking about the ethics of this. Why should the worst produce be given as charity? If one were a Christian, one could make the case that the very best produce should be given as charity. Certainly Jesus went in for that kind of radicalism. And is not the destitute person in greater spiritual need of a perfect melon than the pampered rich woman for whom even perfection is never quite good enough? Having raised the question, I began to be bothered by it, very slightly. It was a puzzle that I hadn't yet thought through.

The usual defect that kicks a melon back into the number two grade is a little hole where a mouse has nibbled on it. That is the sort of melon that I eat myself. I have no quarrels with mice—little pacifist vegetarians with a penchant for domesticity. Cleaning up the barnyard, I'll pick up a board from the ground, and under it find a nest furnished with thistledown and provisioned with barleycorns, a tiny brown face looking up at me. I put the board back, loathe to disturb that tranquil household. Sharing food is everywhere a symbol of peace and friendship, and I consider it a privilege to share a melon with a mouse. So that in giving a mouse-nibbled melon as charity, I am only sharing that very melon that I myself would choose. But it is not a melon that most of my customers would choose, and when I have such a melon at market I sell it for a dollar, less than half the usual price.

It did eventually occur to me that the obvious solution to the ethical dilemma was to let the old Persian woman choose her own melon. I frankly didn't care whether she chose a perfect melon or a mousy one. But when I proposed this to her, by means of a great deal of gesturing and hand-waving, she became coy, and covered her mouth with her hand, and blushed, and wouldn't do it. I was to choose the melon, and she was to choose whatever I would receive in trade.

In the end, I worked out a compromise. I reach into a crate, without looking, and grab whatever melon comes to hand. It might be perfect, it might be a number-two grade. The Persian woman is satisfied with this, and so am I. And it is consistent with a notion that I have always been comfortable with—that the universe is a random place in which the spears of fate are flung aimlessly by a blindfolded god.

We Eat Like Peasants

W<small>E EAT LIKE PEASANTS, WHATEVER'S AT HAND.</small> An hour before dinner, I find myself rummaging in the garden, a few fennels tucked under my arm, my hat full of beans, tugging leeks out of the ground—ought to be able to make something out of that. On our place we grow olives, lemons, and figs; persimmons, mandarins, and apricots; prunes, nectarines, and grapes; tomatoes, peppers, and eggplant; fennel, radicchio, and artichokes; lettuces, carrots, and beets; squash, okra, and pumpkins; and a number of other things which I can't recall at the moment. Some is intended for commerce, some for the use of the house. A manager with an MBA would be appalled by the seemingly haphazard plan of our farm, and by the unfathomable calendar according to which we operate. But he needn't worry. It's more or less under control.

The list of crops, together with the etceteras, suggests a varied diet, and in the course of a year this is so. But in the course of any given week, there is much less variation. The characteristic feature of a peasant diet is that today's menu is the same as yesterday's menu is the same as tomorrow's menu. Here's a sample of our lunches from July. Monday: tomatoes with basil, grilled aubergine on toast, apricots. Tuesday: tomatoes with basil, grilled aubergine on toast, apricots. Wednesday: tomatoes with basil, grilled aubergine on toast, apricots. Thursday: tomatoes with basil, grilled aubergine on toast, apricots. This changes slowly through the year, so that by October the grilled aubergine has given way to a sardine, and the apricot has been replaced by a persimmon, and maybe there are some new potatoes with mustard seeds alongside.

Here's the curious thing. Not only is this diet not monotonous, but with the passage of time it tastes better and better. The Mexican villager who has been eating tortillas and beans and salsa every day for seventy years finds them more satisfying than they were ten years ago. And the old Malay fisherman relishes his rice and fish with lime more than he did in his youth. With enough repetitions, a certain perfection creeps into things. The pianist who begins her daily practice by playing some of Bach's Goldberg Variations finds that after thirty years she has not become tired of the piece. Indeed, it continues to reveal new depths. This is not just because of the complexity of the relationships between each note and all the other notes. It also has to do with the ten thousand previous performances, some on joyful days, others on grievous ones, which have somehow permeated the score so that every phrase is laden with layers of memory. And our lunch of tomatoes with basil and grilled aubergine on toast is similarly freighted. It is not just a July lunch, it is also an unconscious echo of all those other Julys, the ones before we had children, when things were simpler, and then when the children were small and their little faces crumpled into dismay and betrayal at their first taste of aubergine. We're not actively thinking of these things at lunch; but they are an unacknowledged condiment that flavors the experience.

This is not to disparage novelty, which has its place. Like most peasants, we look forward to our holidays and feast days and gatherings with friends, and enjoy them as much in anticipation as in actuality. And if a new Thai restaurant opens in town, we're sure to check it out. But these occasions have to be well spaced if they are to maintain the proper counterpoint to our mundane dinners. It seems to me that an unmuzzled compulsion to seek novelty is a mistake. The food enthusiast who travels to the remotest part of the earth searching for an unheard-of dish with which to jolt his jaded palate is missing something he could have got by staying at home. And that is the subtle and cumulative pleasure of eating like a peasant.

Mrs. K.

Mrs. K. was married to Mr. K., who owned the bank. Although Mr. K. was a wealthy man, Mrs. K. had more money than he did. Her family had been pioneers in the region, and her grandfather Sumner had owned four thousand acres. Over the years the land had been subdivided and pieces sold off, at great profit, and now Mrs. K. owned only a twenty-acre block with a fine old house on it that had been her Aunt Thelma's place. There was a homestead orchard there—a few trees each of dozens of varieties of apples and pears, apricots and plums, nectarines and peaches, mandarins and oranges. The orchard had been planted eighty years ago, and no one still lived who remembered the names of the varieties, nor was that written down anywhere. So when Mrs. K. brought bags of fruit to her friends, which was about ten months out of the year, she would say, "I have some special plums for you," or, "I have some special pears for you." Special because they weren't the kind sold in the store, but she didn't know their names.

One of Mrs. K's friends said to her one day, "You should go to the farmers' market with all this fruit." The idea took root, and in a few months Mrs. K. had secured the necessary permits and certificates, and she became a market vendor.

The day before a market day, Mrs. K. would walk through the orchard, studying the trees and tasting fruit. When she found a tree, or perhaps just one branch of a tree, that she wished picked, she tied a pink ribbon around it. The two Mexicans who did the outdoor work, Hector and Ignacio, dragged their ladders through the orchard and picked the fruit wherever there was a ribbon. They took it to the barn, washed it piece by piece, and set it out on tables to dry. Mrs. K. would inspect the fruit, rejecting the imperfect pieces, and then Hector and Ignacio would pack what had not been rejected in shallow boxes and load them into the trunk of Mrs. K.'s Mercedes. On market day Mrs. K., dressed in blue jeans and a chambray shirt, would drive the Mercedes to market and set out her boxes of fruit on a couple of card tables. On the fourth finger of her left hand she wore a diamond the size of a grape, and she wore a diamond watchband, and a diamond necklace, and diamond earrings. "What's the point in having jewels if they're locked up in the vault all the time," she thought. "Better to wear them." However, she refrained from wearing a diamond tiara to market, which she knew would be out of place, though it was very beautiful.

Sometimes at the farmers' market I would be assigned a spot adjacent to Mrs. K., and over the course of a couple of years I got some inkling of what she was about. I don't think she was there for the money. Indeed, Mrs. K.'s notion of price had been fixed when she first became a homemaker and began shopping, about 1955. She charged forty cents a pound for all of her fruit, favoring that price because it made it easy to calculate the value of half-pounds and quarter-pounds. Partly she came to market because she was sociable and loved to talk, and partly she was there to share—and also show off—the marvelous old varieties of fruit. But more than that, she wanted people to know who she was. The region was growing so rapidly, and so many strangers were moving in, that hardly anyone knew the significance of her family name, although Sumner Road was a major artery. So she asked people where they lived, and if it happened that they lived in the Willow Creek subdivision, she would tell them how that land had belonged to her grandfather Sumner, who'd had four thousand acres in town. And if they didn't live in Willow Creek, she'd tell them anyway.

On a particular Saturday that I am thinking of, the north wind was blowing hard. In our district, the north wind is an evil wind. It scours the Canadian wasteland, gathering strife and grief, which it carries to us. When the north wind blows, few venture out. So there were hardly any customers at the market, though all the farmers were there, including Mrs. K.

I was set up next to a man named Ray Martinez, who had driven to market in his ailing '64 Chevy pickup with a load of apricots. He had beautiful fruit of a variety called Hungarian Rose, in which the side of the fruit facing the sun is crimson, and the other side golden. The apricots were certified organic. He was charging a dollar a pound for them. It was past ten o'clock; the market was already more than half over, and he had sold barely thirty dollars' worth of fruit.

"I don't know what I'm going to do, Mike," he said. "I'm hardly going to cover my gas today. I have so many unpaid bills at home, I don't know where to start. They already cancelled my homeowner's insurance; I just hope the place doesn't burn down. My property tax is up to a 20 percent penalty now. I have to pay that. I was going to pay it with my Visa card, but there wasn't enough credit. I'm so far behind on payments to the orthodontist that I didn't dare take my daughter in to get her braces tightened last time, and now they keep calling. Think maybe they'd take a few hundred pounds of apricots in payments?" He laughed. "I already cut my boy's clarinet lessons back to once a month. He's a whiz on that thing; maybe he can just teach himself.

"The funny thing is," he said, "I have great fruit this year. Best crop in years. And I just can't get it sold, not retail, not wholesale."

Ray looked down the aisle to where Mrs. K. was selling apricots of no known name for forty cents a pound. Her diamonds winked in the sunlight. Some Chinese students held bags bulging with apricots, waiting for them to be weighed. And instead of weighing the fruit, Mrs. K. was telling them very earnestly about her grandfather Sumner, who had owned four thousand acres in town, and the Chinese students were looking at her with utter incomprehension. Ray said aloud, to no one in particular, "Why is that woman here?"

Mark, the Melon Man

I WAS SETTING UP MY DISPLAY on a Wednesday afternoon, dragging buckets of flowers out of the van, when I heard the distinctive putt-putt of a tiny diesel engine. Looking down the street I saw what appeared to be a heap of melons moving slowly along. They bounced up the curb and glided to a stop in the market. It was Mark, the melon man.

Mark grew melons about forty-five miles away, in Yuba City, and he had the most inappropriate vehicle imaginable—a tiny diesel Volkswagen Rabbit. When he was loading for market he would first load the backseat and trunk right to the roof, and then the passenger seat as well, leaving a little place for the driver. He then loaded melons into net bags, the kind that a coach keeps a dozen soccer balls in. He filled these bags in pairs of about equal weight, and tied them together and hung them across the roof so they were balanced, the way that you would load a mule. He hung them side to side and fore and aft until the little car disappeared under a heap of melons except for the driver's half of the windshield.

The car loaded in this way was flagrantly illegal, and Mark had figured out a route to the market that avoided public roads. He would drive along the seasonal dirt farm roads that ring each field; when he came to a paved road he would wait until there were no cars, and then shoot across. About eight miles from his place he would pick up a maintenance right-of-way along some high voltage lines and follow this for a dozen miles. Then he would cut across a couple of fields and pick up a track that paralleled an irrigation canal. After a few miles this intersected the railroad, where he would turn to the left and follow the tracks to the edge of town. Here he had to sneak through some deserted residential neighborhoods, and then shoot down some back alleys to market.

Mark was a carefree, happy fellow, tall and handsome and unambitious, full of jokes. Melons were the perfect crop for him, for there is something innately happy about them. At the market Mark would juggle cantaloupes, and balance a honeydew on his elbow, and clown around with Crenshaws, and waltz with a watermelon. Even grumpy people couldn't suppress a smile when they passed his stand.

Judging the ripeness of a melon is a tricky business, heavily laden with superstition. Mark was happy to share his methods with curious customers. You judge a cantaloupe, or any other melon with a netted rind, by smelling it; it should be richly fragrant, and it should slightly yield to pressure from your thumb on the end where the stem was attached. You tell the ripeness of a honeydew by shaking it next to your ear and listening. If the seeds are loose inside and sloshing around, then it's ripe. If they are held tight, then the melon is green, and it will never ripen. For a watermelon, find the spot that was against the ground when the melon lay in the field. If the spot is greenish or white, the melon is unripe; if it is yellowish, the melon is ready. Thumping watermelons and listening to the sound is hokum.

At the end of the market, Mark would stack the unsold melons, if there were any, for the senior gleaners who picked up excess produce for the county food bank. He then climbed into his car, which now seemed as spacious as a limousine, and drove home on the public roads.

Crooked Is Good

I WAS POKING AROUND IN THE WAREHOUSE at Sac Valley Box one day, in search of wooden boxes to pack pomegranates in, when I came across a pile of foam rubber sheets with tiny dimples in them. The old guy who runs the place explained to me that they were for shipping cherries to Japan. Each cherry is wrapped in a little square of tissue paper, and then set into its foam rubber nest for the voyage.

That a cherry would be individually wrapped, and individually sold (at an extortionate price) seems extreme, and yet it shows an appealing sensitivity and respect. This is not fruit to be gobbled by the handful, but to be placed in a special bowl on a special table and to be studied and appreciated and admired and contemplated before, finally, being tasted. Those of us who find ourselves needing to pick another two hundred pounds before sundown cannot give each cherry the attention it deserves. But we like to think that our customers can take that time.

But there is another, sinister, side to Japanese fruit marketing. That is the idea that every piece of fruit must be perfect—unblemished and symmetrical. Every cherry must be the archetypal cherry, every plum the archetypal plum. Friends of mine who export produce to Japan are driven crazy by the requirement that each vegetable or piece of fruit conform *exactly* to an arbitrary standard. This is a rigid and intolerant view of the world, rather like the view that every young woman must look like, let us say, Barbie. I wouldn't want every young woman to look like Barbie (even one might be too many); a beaky nose, a gap between the front teeth, asymmetric eyebrows become charms and endearments when they pertain to your friends.

I once visited a packing shed in California where potatoes were being sorted. If you have ever grown potatoes, you will know that they are full of notions. This one has a furrowed brow, that one is subject to depressions, and then you'll find a whole nest that have decorated themselves with bumps and knobs. The packers were recognizing five grades: culls, number twos, number ones, potatoes for the military (which were a slightly higher grade than number ones), and finally, the apex, the acme, the Miss Americas of the potatoes, were labeled "pommes de terre" and wrapped in purple tissue, for sale to restaurants. The prerequisite to become a "pomme de terre" was pure conformity to the archetype, with not a whiff of individuality.

Once at the market I was apologizing to my customer, a young woman, about the crookedness of some snapdragons. She shrugged and said in a heavy Italian accent, "Crooked is good, crooked is good." If I were a single man looking for a wife, there's a woman I would court.

This week I've been harvesting eggplant. We grow a variety called Minifinger, a slender, shiny, black fruit with a green calyx, about the size of a banana, and another one called Millionaire, which is similar except that the calyx is purple and the fruit doesn't take the heat as well, and we also grow a neon pink version of these called Ping Tung. I notice when I'm harvesting that there's always a bit of tension, a bit of conflict, between the aesthetic attraction of a box of perfect and uniform eggplants, and the view that there is virtue in all of them, that a profusion of shapes and sizes is appealing. As it turns out, I harvest nearly all of them, which I think shows me to be a good Democrat. In the market there will be some customers with rigid notions about eggplant who subject themselves to a lifetime of disappointment by their conviction that only one in a hundred is perfect enough. These customers are compensated for by others who think that crooked is good. In the end, all of the eggplant is sold.

Tomato Business

My wife's grandmother's third husband was in the tomato business. I have one of his business cards: "V. T. Hinely, Fresh Produce, Tomatoes a Specialty." Twice a week for forty-some years, he would leave Savannah, Georgia, in the evening and drive his flatbed truck to the tomato fields around Ruskin, Florida. There he would buy a truckload of tomatoes in the small hours of the morning and turn back to Savannah, arriving at his warehouse at dawn.

At my wedding, after the ceremony, people were just standing around, and V. T. pulled me off to one side and said, "You're a married man, now. No more fooling around." I looked at his face to see if he was joking, but he seemed pained and embarassed. I'm sure his wife put him up to it; after three husbands and who knows what all else, she probably had a low opinion of men. I thanked him for his advice, and then there was an awkward silence while we wondered what to say next.

Finally I asked, "So what kind of trucks did you drive back and forth to Ruskin?"

He seemed relieved to have a viable topic of conversation. "Well, I started out with a Chevrolet, and then a Diamond T and a Brockway and a Studebaker, and finally another Chevy. That Brockway was sprung way too stiff for tomatoes—beat 'em up. I kept it less than a year. The Studebaker had a nice gentle ride, though."

He took my arm and pulled me closer, as if he were about to tell me a profound family secret. "I sold potatoes and onions and lettuce and carrots, too. I just got those things at the wholesale terminal in Savannah. All the other produce guys got them there, too, and paid the same price I did, so selling those things was very competitive, and it was hard to make a profit. But the tomatoes at the wholesale terminal weren't that great. I was the only one who made the effort to go to Ruskin and get great tomatoes. All the restaurants knew that I had the best tomatoes in town, and as long as I was delivering tomatoes, they'd buy all that other stuff from me, too. So I was able to shut out all those other guys selling to restaurants."

V. T. leaned closer, ready to impart to me, the newest family member, the sum of the wisdom he had gained over seventy-five years. "Don't ever underestimate a tomato," he said.

October 7

File September spray reports, olives
Call in October notice of intent to spray
Mail in property tax
Stake chrysanthemums
Repair coyote damage to irrigation – apricots
Repair irrigation – citrus
Harvest winter melons – move to barn
Mow old melon beds
Disk empty beds
Pick up bell beans, oats, clover seed
Fertilize gerbera with Osmocote
Order gypsum for citrus, persimmons
Replace tractor alternator
Change oil in the Honda
Eighty bouquets for market
Forty bunches of sunflowers to Nugget
Propagate curly willow
Collect seed: okra, echinops, tomatoes, solanum
Save seed from Piel de Sapo melons
Take dead hawk in the freezer to the zoology museum
Order twenty-five tons compost for beds
Find out about getting rice hulls delivered
Sixty stems of tuberose for wedding
Pot up some crinadonna for market
Divide watsonia before it's too late
Mow, disk south field; prepare to plant beans
Start sweet peas
Sow pansies, greenhouse
Move delphinium seedlings up to 72's
Plant out calendula
Plant out campanula
Plant out stocks
Replace broken flail, small mower
Plant out Stockton red onions

Margot

I ONCE SPOKE TO MARGOT ON THE PHONE, but I never met her. She was looking for land to lease, and had got hold of my name and called me. I had enough acreage available, but I couldn't guarantee an adequate supply of water, so she ended up renting someplace else.

I was vaguely aware that she had a farm going in the district. I heard her name from time to time, and then after a while I didn't hear her name anymore, and figured she had gone away. It was only several years after she had left town that I heard her story from a friend of mine who had worked for her.

Margot was from a prominent Boston family with plenty of money, and had grown up in the East. I don't know what brought her here, or if she had any background in farming, but she came to our district to take a job as an apprentice on a little organic farm. She was a dynamo—smart and industrious and full of energy and ideas. Within three months she was manager of the farm, and at the end of the year she decided to strike out and start farming on her own. That's when I had the phone call from her.

She leased land, leased a couple of tractors, put up a greenhouse, and hired workers. She grew vegetables and salad greens over an eleven-month season, and developed contracts with restaurants around Sacramento, and sold at farmers' markets and at an upscale greengrocer's. She seemed to know exactly what she was doing and had the self-confidence to charge high prices. A fearless negotiator, she made large promises and kept her word. The first year, she had

$250,000 in sales, and the second year she doubled that. In our community there were some small farmers who did well and some who did poorly, but we were all more or less in the same league. And then Margot came along and brought an entirely new yardstick with which to measure the business of farming, and by that measure all of us were thinking too small.

However shrewd Margot was in business, she was an innocent in affairs of the heart. She fell in love with one of her workers, a Mexican man named Narciso who was an illegal alien. He was slender and shy, with shiny black hair hanging over his eyes and skin the color of chocolate. Narciso was eighteen years old; Margot was thirty-six. He spoke no English, and she spoke no Spanish. But at a certain level of animal chemistry, love thrives without words; it is nourished enough by lingering glances, and subtle movements of the eyebrows, and moistened lips, and the gentle touch of skin on skin. Over a period of weeks, the other workers watched with amusement the escalating gazes of Narciso and Margot, and their steady abandonment of discretion. One Monday Narciso remarked that over the weekend he had moved into Margot's apartment.

In December Narciso went back to Mexico to visit his parents. Margot was lovelorn and distracted, and moped around the greenhouse, worrying that he might not find his way back. In January she told the crew that she was going to drive to Tijuana and bring Narciso across the border in the trunk of her car. The workers pleaded with her to give up this unwise plan, but she went anyway. They were intercepted at the border. Narciso was sent back to Mexico, and Margot's car was impounded by the Immigration and Naturalization Service.

Later that day, Narciso walked across the border and met Margot in a restaurant, and the two of them took a taxi to the San Diego airport and bought tickets to Sacramento. But he was intercepted in the airport and sent back to Mexico, and Margot came home alone. A week later Narciso showed up at the farm.

Within a few days they had gone to the county seat and been married by a justice of the peace. With marriage license in hand, they went to see an immigration lawyer about getting a green card for Narciso. "Let me interview each of you separately," said the lawyer. First he interviewed Margot; then he interviewed Narciso. Then he called Margot back in again. "It's not going to work," he said. "Narciso has a wife and two children in Mexico. If you'd like, I can help you get an annulment."

So the marriage was annulled, but they kept living together. And by June it was obvious that Margot was pregnant. A little chocolate-colored baby girl was born in November and named Angelina, with Margot's last name. Narciso went back to Mexico in December and did not return. Margot was preoccupied with Angelina and didn't seem to notice Narciso's absence.

That year there was a strong El Niño current in the Pacific, and it was the rainiest winter in half a century. The greenhouse was filled with seedlings on top of the benches and seedlings under the benches and seedlings in the aisles, and there was no possibility of planting them out, for the ground was too wet to work up any beds. The workers bumbled around in the greenhouse, moving root-bound seedlings into bigger flats, waiting for a break in the weather that seemed like it might never come. The fifteen-day forecast was for fifteen more days of rain. One of the workers said, "Margot, there's fungus starting to spread through the tomatoes and peppers."

The workers stood in a clump in the aisle, listening to the rain on the greenhouse roof, waiting for a decision, waiting for instructions. Margot looked up at the greenhouse roof, at the trickles of water dripping from leaky seams, and said quietly, "I quit." She sat down in a plastic chair and unbuttoned her blouse and set Angelina to nursing, and then she pulled out her checkbook and wrote out paychecks for the workers. Two days later she and Angelina flew back to Boston, and the workers drifted off to other jobs. So far as I know, she never returned here.

From our perspective, Margot was a strange phenomenon, like the El Niño current. She blew into town without warning, upsetting the order of things and upsetting our assumptions, and then, as suddenly, she was gone. From the perspective of her family and friends in Boston, it must have seemed that Margot went away for three years and then came home again, with a small brown baby. As for Narciso, I imagine him still a farmworker, prematurely aged, crouching in a muddy field, picking strawberries, thinking idly about a magical year when he lived in a spacious apartment with a beautiful red-haired woman with whom he shared no words. About Margot's perspective I can only guess. Perhaps she was swept away by the pro-creative urge that can strike women at that age, an urge that brought forth heaps of cabbages and overflowing bins of tomatoes and a small brown baby. And then that urge subsided, and Margot went back to her old life. But the perspective that interests me most of all is that of Angelina. I can imagine her leading a life of privilege in Boston, admired by her friends for her exotic coloring. Once in a while she says to her mother, "Mom, tell me again who my father was, and how you met him, and how it was that I came to be."

Board of Directors Meeting

IN ANY GROUP OF PEOPLE that holds formal meetings there will always be at least one nonstop talker. In our group—the board of directors of the local farmers' market—it was Wes, an old almond farmer. All day long, out there on his tractor, he rehearsed and stored up conversation, packing it away until it was under so much pressure that when he got the floor at the board meeting he couldn't be shut off. Wes' narrative reminded me of the way a crop duster spraying a ten-acre field needs about fifteen thousand acres to maneuver in. His line of talk would climb into the distance, getting farther and farther from the topic, and then it would make a broad turn, and line itself up, and pretty soon we could see, "Ah yes, here it comes, he's heading back toward the field of discussion." Slouched in his chair, his hair swept back as if by the wind, his hands spinning like propellers, Wes would steer his monologue back to the subject, deliver a quick blast of pertinent comment as he passed overhead, and then away he would go, zooming off in another direction. On this night, we were discussing whether to admit a vendor of sugar-coated popcorn to the market. We sat weary but mesmerized, staring at the paper plates and pizza crusts and half-empty cans of Mountain Dew while Wes, at the apogee of his narrative's course, talked about why it was important for a wholesale tomato grower to wear a straw hat when he called on his clients. Wes stopped to take a drink of water, and choked on it, and Boris the baker seized the floor.

Boris had the look of a Maurice Sendak baker, with his floury, doughy body bulging out of his clothes in many places, straining the belts and buttons. "I don't know why we're having this discussion," he said. "It's obvious that this is a synergistic thing. The more vendors we have, the more people come to the market, and then we all do better. All those children there with their mothers, they want that popcorn. They're going to say to their moms, 'Hey, let's go to the farmers' market,' because they're thinking about popcorn, and once they're there, the moms will buy all kinds of other stuff."

"But Boris," somebody said, "the person who's just spent six bucks on a bag of popcorn has six dollars less to spend on tomatoes, or peaches, or flowers. This Wednesday night market is turning into a circus. The total revenues are up, but not the farmers' revenues. And another thing: this sugar-coated popcorn is garbage, it's antithetical to the notion of real food, and isn't that what we stand for?"

Boris scoffed. "People come to the market with plenty of money," he said, "and if they run out, they go to the ATM and get more. Just because they bought popcorn is not in any way going to decrease their purchases of other things. It's so simple, why can't you see it? The more people we bring in, the more we sell. And the more we sell, the more money we make. And more money is better, right?"

"Wrong!" boomed out a deep voice, and at the same instant a huge brown hand slapped the table. We looked around. It was Octavio, who almost never speaks at these meetings. "More money is not better, Boris. If we thought that, none of us would be farmers. The money's just incidental." Octavio pointed a finger at Boris. "According to your logic, we should bring a pornography vendor into the market. Maybe some of those perverts would get hungry, and come buy some bagels from you. Is this what we want? No. It's not about money. It's about integrity."

We had never heard Octavio speak at such length, and now the room was silent. I looked at Boris. He was staring straight down at the table, and his face was crimson. He was not chastised, he was furious. For Boris is an upright man. He writes generous checks to many charities. He serves on the boards of several not-for-profit organizations, he donates bread to the poor. He even travels to third world countries at his own expense, to teach bakers there how to modernize their bakeries. That some dirt farmer should criticize his integrity was intolerable.

It occurred to me that I was watching a clash of two philosophies that in every culture coexist uneasily. On the one hand is the merchant who is also a man of God, ruthless in the marketplace but generous in society. It is a common caricature among Quakers and Jews, Arabs and Chinese, Scots and Calvinists. Such a one reckons that his life's deeds are like scraps of paper in a basket, some with pluses and some with minuses, and that if they are dumped out on the table and sorted by type, as long as the pluses predominate he is in God's favor. On the other hand are Octavio and his kindred, who believe that in life there is only one moment, the Eternal Now, and that moment demands righteous action. This is a philosophy that would be congenial to Kant and to Kierkegaard, and to Jesus and to Buddha. Octavio embraced this notion unthinkingly. He was known to all of us as a good-willed and generous man who could be counted on to do the right thing. His pound of apricots weighed at least twenty ounces, and if it cost a dollar and a quarter, he would wave away the quarter and let the dollar be enough. He would never be rich. And this, perhaps, is a point in favor of Boris and his kind, for they are the ones who endow universities and libraries and symphonies and museums and orphanages and hospitals. They are pillars of society in a way that Octavio could not be.

I think that most of the farmers in the room sided with Octavio. There is something about farming, perhaps the unpredictability of the weather, that tends to make farmers into existentialists. But as much as it was a farmer-vs.-baker issue, it was also a country person–vs.–city person issue. The city dweller is surrounded in every dimension by human artifacts and enterprises that seem to fill the universe. But to a farmer, standing in his barnyard—his view encompassing a cloudy sky, a field of wheat, some chickens scratching under an apricot tree—the city is but a smudge on the horizon, and its preoccupation with business, so urgent to the urbanite, is of no consequence.

Charlie broke the silence first. "Mr. Chairman," he said, "I'd like to make an amendment to the motion that's on the floor." We looked questioningly around at one another. None of us is a parliamentarian, and our aping of the rules of order is haphazard, at times bordering on comical. None of us knew if a motion could be amended or not.

"Go ahead, Charlie," said the chairman.

"I'd like to change the motion so that it goes like this: I move that the popcorn vendor be admitted to the market under the condition that he provide the manager with a producer's certificate signed by the agriculture commissioner verifying that he has himself grown the corn from which his popcorn is made." Somebody seconded the motion. We all knew that the popcorn guy didn't grow his own corn. He was just a city dweller who had bought a franchise for sugar-coated popcorn. But the motion was a good one; it would effectively bar him from the market without necessarily barring the concept of popcorn.

Wes grabbed the floor, revved up his propellers, and made a few acrobatic passes around the new motion, relating it to commodity marketing, and to the recycling of Styrofoam cups, and to recent findings on the health benefits of olive oil, but the chairman managed to cut him off. When the motion came to a vote it passed, with only Boris the baker dissenting.

Rob Swenson

Rob Swenson had some kind of genetic or metabolic abnormality that made it impossible for him to gain weight, no matter how much he ate. Though he was as tall as I am, I don't think he weighed a hundred and ten pounds. All of Rob's surfaces were concave, giving him a gaunt look, and yet he was not unhandsome, with soft brown eyes and a blond ponytail. Nor was he weak—he had the surprising strength of people who are all bone and sinew.

When he was a child, Rob's odd appearance attracted the attention of the school bullies. They threw his homework in the ditch, and his books in the ditch, and sometimes they threw him in the ditch. He never said as much, but I expect that that experience had something to do with his dim view of society.

I had known Rob for years, long before either of us had much to do with farming. His girlfriend of the time was an acquaintance of mine, and she introduced us, and we became friends. Rob and I had a lot in common. We both rejected the values of the dominant culture in which we lived and expressed this in a deep sense of irony. Neither of us had ever owned a television. Neither of us used credit nor had any debts. Neither of us had ever been a member of a group—not Cub Scouts, or Boy Scouts, or Little League, or the Young Republicans, or the Unitarian church, or the Studebaker drivers' club, or the Lions Club, or the Green Party, or even the Farm Bureau. We were not outcasts, because we had never been *in* anything to be cast out of, but we were outsiders, voluntary exiles at home, intramural aliens. We shared a strong sense of not belonging, and possibly of being unwelcome.

In all of this, Rob was more extreme than I. He had no social security number and had never registered for the draft, nor was he registered to vote. He had no bank account, no credit card, and no insurance, owned no land, and had almost no possessions beyond a Honda motorcycle, a piano, and a few threadbare changes of clothes. And he filed no tax returns, though his income as a shade-tree Volvo mechanic probably wasn't enough to put him in the mini-mum tax bracket anyway. His business came to him by word of mouth; he was honest and competent and didn't charge much, and satisfied customers told their Volvo-owning friends. Rob also took on cars that no one else would touch—Packards and Ramblers and Fiats. If someone needed a new clutch in their Hudson Hornet, they would eventually come across Rob's name, and he'd take care of them. He accepted work when he was in the mood or broke, and didn't when he wasn't, and that left him plenty of time to play his piano, and ride his motorcycle, and sit under a tree and watch clouds. He had discovered the value of simplicity long before it became a trendy movement for overwrought yuppies.

The place Rob rented was on an acre and a half, and it had about forty pear trees. The landlord said they were Bartletts, but they didn't look like it to me—small, pale yellow, sweet pears with melt-ing flesh. It was some old variety, orphaned and forgotten, and the fruit was excellent. The trees were unirrigated, though about a third of them were over the leach field of the septic system, and those were always happier looking.

Rob was oblivious to the trees except when the fruit was ripe, in autumn, and then for a few weeks he would harvest pears and take them to the market. I couldn't stand to see the trees untended, and so the rest of the year I took charge of managing them. I'd come by with a ladder and some loppers and a bucket of bleach and bang on the door. "Come on," I'd say. "There's fire blight in the pear trees, and we need to prune it out." And he'd come out and we'd spend the afternoon pruning the wilted branches out of the trees and taking them to the burn pile. Or if I came by in late spring and noticed too much fruit, I'd conscript Rob, and we'd thin the fruit, trying to keep the little pears about four inches apart so they'd have enough room to grow. He was a steady and cheerful worker, but he wouldn't have done these things if I hadn't brought them up. In fall, when I was sowing clover in my own orchards, I'd stop by with a bag of clover seed and scatter it out among the pears as well.

At the farmers' market Rob was quiet, nearly shy. Being quiet can be more powerful than being loud, and customers were attracted to Rob and to his pears. If he had been an ambitious man, he could have propagated the trees, and leased or bought land, and planted out a large acreage, and hired workers, and made a lot of money with those pears. It's what I might have done. But his ambitions didn't tend in that direction. He took the pears as they came, and that was enough.

Of all the freedoms that the politicians blather about, there is one that is almost never mentioned, although it outranks the others. And with every decade it is more elusive, and fewer and fewer enjoy it. Rob was one of those few, and the freedom he took for himself was the freedom not to participate in society. Some would criticize Rob for being unambitious, and for turning down useful work if he weren't in the mood for working. But he did not consume much, either goods or services. In the balance, his contributions surely outweighed his debits, and I would rate him as a good citizen, in spite of himself—an odd epithet for an anarchist.

The Road to Venus

To PLANT A VINEYARD IS EASIER than to tear it out five years later when you've changed your mind. I've been reflecting on this lately while digging out grapevines. A few years ago I decided to add a vineyard to my farm, with the idea of growing commercially some of the unusual grapes that are seldom seen outside of specialist's collections. The usual market grape in this area is Red Flame, a quintessential industrial grape. Its virtues, from the grower's perspective, are great vigor and productivity, good appearance, and fruit that is famous for its durability in cold storage and long-distance shipping. The flavor and texture? Crunchy sugar water.

My criterion in selecting grapes was to be flavor. If the vines were unvigorous, the season short, and the fruit fragile and seedy, I didn't care. Flavor was to be the thing. My quest for flavorful grapes led me to the collection at the University of California, Davis, where I had the opportunity to sample over two hundred and sixty cultivars of table grapes collected from around the world. The vines were laid out alphabetically. I started bravely one September morning with Almeria, tasting and taking notes, and by noon, when I was feeling sick from eating too many grapes, I had made it to Barlinka, the classic table grape of South Africa. I was able to return a few times each week, and in October I finally reached Yargouti. Whatever grape I was eating at the moment always seemed the most wonderful, but I managed to narrow the field down to twenty varieties. I acquired a few bundles of cuttings and planted out a little vineyard of five hundred vines.

Friends of mine in the produce business warned me, "No one will buy grapes with seeds—you're just wasting your time." But I didn't believe them. God gave us molars for a reason. Eighteen of the twenty varieties I planted out had seeds. The seeds themselves have a wonderful peppery flavor when you crunch them in your teeth, adding to the already complex flavor of skin and pulp. The seeds are beautiful, too. When I was a student, a friend was writing his dissertation on fossil grape seeds from a coal mine in Vermont, and he taught me to appreciate their handsome architecture.

As it turned out, the pessimistic produce brokers were right. Grapes with seeds don't sell. True, we have a small band of fanatically loyal customers for Golden Muscat and Rish Baba and Niabell who start phoning us as early as May, wanting to know when the grapes will be ready. But these few enthusiasts couldn't sustain the economics of the vineyard, and so I've been tearing it out. One grape, a seedless one, turned out to be commercially successful, and we have increased our planting of it. This is Venus, a black-skinned grape that is a cross between the European *Vitis vinifera* and the North American *Vitis labrusca*. It has the foxy flavor of a Concord, with some of the lusciousness of a Black Monukka. And it's extremely early, ready for harvest by the Fourth of July, a good three weeks ahead of Flame. Whatever fruit we leave on the vine turns to raisins, which we harvest in September.

If I had only a little garden, with room for just one vine, I wouldn't choose a table grape at all—it would be a wine grape, Cabernet Sauvignon. Perhaps it's lack of imagination, or an overly developed sense of orderliness, that makes people think that wine grapes are only for wine and table grapes only for the table. True, the wine grapes have tiny berries and lots of seeds, and they are so juicy that the juice runs down your chin and all over your shirt, but the flavor of fresh Cabernet grapes is unsurpassed. And if you are patient, and leave some bunches on the vine until they have begun to wither and ferment and are struck by frost, you can enjoy a special treat usually known only to quail and mockingbirds.

Marika

IN AUGUST AND PART OF SEPTEMBER, when apples are in season, an apple grower is next to me at the market. About every tenth customer holds up an apple and says, "An apple a day keeps the doctor away," as if this profound observation had never been made before. If I'm free at that moment, I tell the apple joke. I say, "Yes, and an apple every eight hours keeps *three* doctors away." The customers regard me strangely. I seem to be the only one who finds it funny.

One Wednesday in late September I pulled into my spot at the market and noticed that the apple vendor wasn't there. Apple season was over. In her place, a woman was setting up a display of beautiful dried fruit. There were the usual sorts of things—dried apricots and Mission figs and Thompson seedless raisins. But she also had dried white nectarines and yellow nectarines, and half a dozen varieties of peaches, and pears, and apples, and Calimyrna figs, and golden raisins.

I introduced myself and we shook hands. Her name was Marika, and she spoke with a strong accent that I didn't recognize. "Where are you from?" I asked.

"Petaluma," she said. I raised my eyebrows questioningly. "The farm isn't in Petaluma, though," she went on. "It's down in Tulare County. I actually haven't ever been there myself. I just work for them, doing six farmers' markets a week. They drop off the fruit at a storage place in Petaluma where I pick it up."

At this point a customer interrupted me, and it was an hour later before we could resume our conversation. "So where are you from?" I asked.

"Petaluma," she said.

"No, I mean, you speak with an accent. Where are you from before that?"

"Bulgaria," she said. I had never met anyone from Bulgaria, and had only a hazy notion of what the place was all about.

"So how are things in Bulgaria?" I asked.

She held her hand palm down and toggled it back and forth in a universal gesture meaning "so-so." "Fifty years under the communists were not so good," she said. "Work is very hard to find. That's why I'm here." She paused. "On the other hand, here it is easy to find a job, but people are all stressed out by their work, and take it home with them, and go in on the weekend. At home, you do your job, and at five o'clock you're done, and then you don't think about it anymore and go lead your real life. I think that's better. Americans are very strange about letting their jobs take over their lives.

"My parents have a little farm in a remote place, and so politics and the economy don't faze them much," she said. "But I wanted to get away, at least for a while."

"Would you go back there and work on their farm?" I asked.

"I might," she said. "I'm going back this winter for a visit. I'll see how things are."

A while later there was again a break in commerce, and we found ourselves idle for a moment, and I asked her, "So are people in Bulgaria happy?" Even as I said it, I realized it was a foolish question, but she didn't brush it off.

After a minute she said, "The people who have a talent for happiness are happy, and the rest..." She turned her palms upward and shrugged.

I said, "Just like here."

She said, "Like everywhere."

Bride to Be

Because I grow and sell flowers, I am often approached, usually by the bride to be, with the question "Do you do flowers for weddings?" My answer is equivocal. "What do you have in mind?" I ask. I stall for time, trying to size up the prospect. Even a normally reasonable woman can become quite irrational on the subject of her wedding, and I continue to be amazed by the way in which people fail to understand the distinction between a wedding and a marriage.

If she says, "I'm getting married next month, and you guys always have great flowers. Whatever is in season would be fine—I'm completely flexible on that," then I'm willing to talk. My rules are that she supply her own containers and pick up the flowers at the farm. I don't make corsages, but I'm willing to put together bouquets. And my prices are very reasonable. A wedding with a dozen tables and a buffet and the bride's bouquet and a few other such things might come to eighty dollars. A florist would charge twelve hundred.

But if the bride is already trying to get a bid on flowers eighteen months before the wedding, or if she has a whiny voice, or if she comes to the market clutching a pair of fuchsia-colored shoes and says, "I need flowers to match these shoes," then I reply, "Let me give you the name of a florist who I think can help you out." There is a lot of profiteering that goes on around the fringes of weddings, and the florist will charge a small fortune, but with that kind of woman he will earn his money.

One October day, a woman who had taken my card at the market phoned me at home. "I'm getting married on Saturday, and I'm trying to find some sunflowers. Do you have any?"

"It's the tail end of the season, but we still have a few," I said. "How many do you need?"

"About forty," she said.

"That's no problem," I said.

"How much will they be?" she asked.

"If you can come pick them up, it will be twenty-five bucks," I said.

"The florist was going to charge me three dollars a stem," she said.

I told her how to find my farm, and she arranged to pick up the flowers Thursday afternoon. On Wednesday night she phoned. "I was going to have a local flower grower up here in Grass Valley do most of the flowers, but it turns out she doesn't have that much. Could I get some other flowers from you besides the sunflowers?"

"Sure," I said. "We can take care of you."

The next afternoon the bride and a friend showed up in a Subaru station wagon. The bride was a hard-run thirty-something former hippie with wrinkles under her eyes and a big smile on her face. I got the impression that she hadn't missed many parties over the years, and that drinking and dancing ranked higher with her than going to work or to church.

"This other grower has pretty much flaked out on me," she said.

"Let's take a walk around and I can show you what there is," I said. While we were walking, I asked, "How many tables are there?"

"Fifty-two," she said.

"Good lord!" I said. "How many people are coming to the wedding?"

"About four hundred," she said. "We're going to do some serious partying."

"You seem very calm for organizing a wedding that size."

"I'm not too concerned about everything being just so. I just want everyone to have fun."

"That seems like a very sound attitude to me," I said. "The most important thing is did you get a good husband?"

"Yeah," she said dreamily, "I did."

"Well, congratulations," I said. "That's the main thing. About these flowers: we'll pick what we can, but I'd recommend that you make the table bouquets with lots of foliage. There's nothing wrong with a bouquet that's 80 percent foliage. And there's lots of good foliage up there around Grass Valley—just step into the woods and cut it. There's a little plant with three-parted shiny leaves that's real pretty this time of year—a beautiful scarlet color—don't pick that."

"Yeah, I know about poison oak," she said.

I got some clippers from the barn, and the three of us set to work picking flowers: scabiosa, zinnias, gerbera, alstroemeria, sea oats, gomphrena, marigolds, ageratum, red hibiscus pods, and the beautiful lime-green pods of the South African milkweed. We picked a full carload, and I figured that with foliage it would be enough. "Do you need something special for the bride's bouquet?" I asked.

"Well, I was wondering about that. I haven't made up my mind."

"What are you wearing?"

"A white wedding dress with a red scarf around my neck, and red cowboy boots."

"How about a bouquet of chile peppers?" I asked. "I've got some plants about two feet tall, loaded with fruit. You'll have to pull the foliage off, though, or it will wilt."

"That would be great!" she said. "I love chiles." I walked out to where the chiles were growing and pulled some plants out of the ground, and groomed them a bit, and hosed off the dust. She stuffed them in the back of her Subaru with the other flowers."

"How much do I owe you?" she asked.

"How about eighty dollars?"

"That's a bargain." She handed me four twenties and shook my hand.

"Have fun," I said, as she climbed into her car. I didn't doubt that she would.

Figs

MISSION FIGS TURN DARK PURPLE about two weeks before they're ready to harvest. I check the orchard every day, sliding my hand around a fig and giving it a gentle squeeze. When the figs are soft and have begun to wilt at the neck, it's time to pick them. You don't pick a fig by tugging and twisting, as you would an apple or a plum; you slide your thumb along the branch and press against the side of the stem to push the fig off.

We take figs to market in shallow trays. Some of our customers are so greedy for figs that, having bought a tray, they stand in the market, eyes closed, face turned heavenward, dropping figs into their mouths and groaning with pleasure while the crowd swirls around them. But better yet is to eat a fig from the west side of the tree late in the afternoon when the sun has been warming it, intensifying its wonderful fragrances.

We produce two or three thousand pounds of fresh figs in the early crop each June (the main crop ripens in September), but we harvest less than ten percent of them. The reason is that we are not the only ones interested in dining on figs. The birds are into them as soon as they turn color. They test for ripeness by pecking a hole in the fig. Even when the fruit is ripe, the birds would rather vandalize it than eat it. If they were wonderful birds, toucans for example, I would say to them, "Help yourselves, my friends, take the whole crop. The pleasure of your company is payment enough." But they are not. Most of the vandals are furtive, wretched, gracklish birds which are neither musical nor handsome nor bold. The mockingbird also is a fig wrecker, no doubt figuring—like many musicians—that any amount of bad behavior will be excused by his lovely singing.

Closer to the ground, the quail will occasionally take a fig, but he much prefers grapes, or green peas if there are still any about this late in the season. Likewise the ring-neck pheasant (I started to write "wring-neck pheasant") takes the odd low-hanging fig. The possum is a great fig enthusiast, but a sloppy eater: he chews with his mouth open and smears the fruit around. Mr. Raccoon, on the other hand, is very dainty with a fig, holding it carefully in his little hand and smoothing his whiskers after each bite. One moonlit night when I was out late, tending irrigation, I saw a gray fox among the fig trees: I don't know if she was tasting fruit or scouting for rodents. I have not seen coyote in the orchard, but I have found piles of coyote scat composed of beetle carapaces and rodent bones all cemented together with fig seeds—the remains of a memorable meal if you're a coyote (even more memorable if you're not).

The ground animals take all the figs up to a height of three feet, and the birds take everything from four feet on up. This leaves a band of fruit for me between three and four feet off the ground—most convenient. I don't need to stoop or stretch, and it's an easy harvest.

I suppose I could increase my take by setting snares and erecting scarecrows, or covering the trees with a net, or putting out a device that makes a rude noise every few moments, but I don't plan to take these measures. The trees require almost no care—I don't spray them or fertilize them or prune them or irrigate them—just pass through once a year with the tractor to knock down weeds, and mail in the property tax each November. So, truly, the figs are the fruit of the land, to be shared by all who live there, and I reckon that three hundred pounds is my full entitlement.

Dan Gonzalez

ONE OF MY CUSTOMERS CAME UP TO ME during the market and said, "Try one of these." She held out to me what appeared to be almonds. I took one and tried it. It wasn't an almond at all, it was an apricot kernel. Ordinarily, apricot kernels are both very flavorful and very bitter. My wife puts a few in each jar of apricot jam that she makes, to enhance the flavor. But these had no bitterness to them at all; they were sweet, and so intense that one kernel seemed to have as much flavor as a quarter-pound of dried apricots.

"Wow!" I said. "These are amazing. Who's selling them?"

"Some lady down there on the other side. I've never seen her before."

Toward the end of the market I abandoned my post and walked down to where the apricot kernels were being sold. A middle-aged woman stood behind a card table heaped with little bags of kernels. She was charging three dollars for a four-ounce bag, or ten dollars a pound. I introduced myself. "Where do you grow these?" I asked.

"Just up the road, in Winters. My partner does the growing end of the business."

"Who's that?" I asked.

"Dan Gonzalez," she said. That explained a lot. Dan Gonzalez was a local man who had an extraordinary knack for business. It didn't surprise me at all that he was behind a new agricultural product that no one had heard of and that sold for ten dollars a pound. Mostly he worked in farming, but I knew he was a partner in a hydroseeding business that seeded road cuts for the highway department. He also was a partner in a big hammer mill that converted waste wood—pallets, used cedar shakes, old fencing, orchard prunings—into mulch, which he sold to landscapers. Dan owned orchards around the county and some row-crop land, and he was one of the wealthiest people in the district, but you wouldn't know it to look at him. He wore old clothes, drove an old truck, and lived in a modest little house in the old part of town. When he had extra money, he bought land. And Dan wasn't one of those businessmen who talks on two cell phones at once and is always racing around in a flurry of activity. He owned no cell phone at all, and had an unhurried way of living. You might mistake him for a happily unemployed tradesman.

One day I had to go to town to pick up a registered letter at the post office. It was some legal papers, and I decided to stop at the diner for a cup of coffee while I studied them. As I pulled into the lot, Dan pulled in right behind me. We greeted each other, and I said, "Dan, let me buy you a cup of coffee. I want to ask you about something."

We got our coffee, and pie, and settled into a booth. "Tell me about these apricot kernels," I said. "I grow apricots, Golden Amber is the variety, but the kernels are so bitter you can't eat them."

"You've tried those, have you?" he asked. "Aren't they good? I remembered them from when I was a kid. They come from an old orchard out on Road 85B that was planted years ago by Achilles Fong. Did you know him?"

"I knew his son, Genghis. Drove a turquoise-blue bullet-nose Studebaker with whitewall tires."

"That's the one. Anyway, Achilles had planted this forty-acre block with some special kind of apricots from China that had sweet seeds. I never knew the name of the variety. I wish I did. He dried all the fruit. Had some kind of contract with the military. Not a great price, but I don't think he cared. He was after the seeds. In China they were considered very special. I believe he had a good business going there.

"After he died that land was bought by a rich woman from Sacramento. She moved to France not too long after that and hired Lee Fairweather to manage the place for her. Well, as you know, it's possible to invent a great many expenses for an orchard, and the place ran at a loss year after year—a loss for the owner that is, not for Lee. Finally she fired him, and the orchard was abandoned. After a couple of years I checked at the county to see if it was coming up for auction for unpaid taxes, but the taxes were all paid.

"Last fall I got the owner's address in France and I wrote to her. I said I wanted to rent that orchard on a five-year lease, and I'd pay the property tax plus a cash rent of fifteen hundred dollars a year. I told her that the trees were half dead with neglect but I'd put it back into shape. Sometimes it's hard to do business with someone seven thousand miles away, so I made it easy for her. I enclosed a check for fifteen hundred dollars, and I wrote the contract right on the check, so that when she signed the check she also signed the contract. She signed it and it came right back to me.

"What set me going on this is that I'd had a phone call from a guy down in Modesto who makes baby food—the kind that comes in little jars. He'd lost one of his suppliers of organic apricots and was looking for a source. There aren't many organic apricots around, and he was offering two hundred dollars a ton premium. I told him to give me a month. That's when I contacted the lady in France. As soon as I got the lease on that place, I tried to get it certified organic. Since it hadn't been sprayed or fertilized in the four years that it had been abandoned, I figured that would constitute organic farming. The CCOF wouldn't go for it, but an agency up in Oregon agreed to certify it for me. So I called the baby-food guy and told him that I could supply organic apricots, but there were conditions. Modesto is a long way to haul that fruit, and freight would be expensive, and I wanted some compensation. Specifically, I wanted him to pay me to haul away the apricot pits, and I wanted the pits from my apricots kept separate from the others. He said he was already paying twelve dollars a ton to have the pits hauled away, and he'd be glad to turn that over to me.

"This first year, it went pretty well. I got the orchard put into shape, and we had an adequate crop, considering. I trucked fruit down to Modesto and trucked pits back. The pits that weren't mine I ran through my hammer mill and sold them as mulch, twenty-five dollars a yard. I had the pits from Achilles' old orchard hauled to some land I own where there was an old almond sheller in a shed. We fiddled and fiddled with that thing, trying to get it to crack apricot pits, and we finally got it to where we would get about 70 percent whole kernels. That was the best we could do. I sent samples of the broken-up stuff to bakeries in the Bay Area to see if I could find a market for that, but I haven't heard back from them.

"I found a Chinese grocery down in Union City that wanted to buy kernels in bulk, and I sell to them, but I wanted to get a farmers' market deal going, too. There's a woman that I know from church, Katie Sullivan, she's the one selling at the market. She's a single mother, had a hard go of it, her ex-husband never paid his child support. She worked at the packinghouse during the season and did some housecleaning the rest of the year, but I don't think she ever had two nickels to rub together. They're good people, Katie and her daughter, and I wanted to do something for them. So I asked her if she wanted to go into business with me as a partner. I'd supply the kernels, she'd sell them, and we'd split the gross fifty-fifty. You know, I have no employees. I only do partnerships and contracts. The labor's more expensive that way, but the amount of headaches that it saves with the state and with workers' compensation is worth it to me.

"So Katie's been selling at six farmers' markets a week for about two months. We give out a lot of free samples, and word is getting around. Our sales increase about 30 percent a week. And Katie's making twice the income that she ever did before. My share of it, fifty percent of retail, is about what I get wholesale from the Chinese man in Union City, so I'm happy with it."

The waitress came around with coffee, and we each took another half a cup.

"This sounds like a typical Dan Gonzalez deal," I said. "It seems to me that you're being paid three times for the same apricot pit: the first time when you sell the fruit in Modesto, the second time when you haul the pits back here, and the third time when you sell the kernels."

"Actually, after we get the kernels out, there's still the broken shells left, and we run those through the hammer mill and sell them for mulch." Dan looked pleased with himself, as if he had told an especially amusing joke.

"You know," he said, "I drive up and down these backcountry roads, and I look to the left and I look to the right, and every place I look I see opportunities just hanging there, waiting for someone to pick them. I pick maybe one out of twenty, because it interests me. The other nineteen I leave for somebody else. All these other farmers, they whine and complain about how tough farming is, and how expensive water is, and how hard it is to make a living. They drive up and down the same roads I do, and they look to the left and they look to the right, and they don't see a thing."

Mowing in the Orchard

HORTICULTURE COULD BE THOUGHT OF AS THE ART of encouraging the growth of some plants while discouraging the growth of others. In my orchards, at ground level, the trunks of the trees occupy only a small part of the area. The citrus trees are spaced on a grid of twelve feet by fifteen, the olives are eleven by eighteen, and the apricots are twenty by twenty. This leaves quite a bit of room for plants that are not the intended crop, and tending the incidental plants takes as much energy as tending the trees themselves.

One year I was reading some books about farming by Masanobu Fukuoka, a Japanese farmer. He grew citrus (mandarins) and he advocated doing nothing at all to tend the orchard floor: let the weeds grow as they would, and if they got to be eight feet tall, so much the better. He made a convincing case for this approach, and I was inspired by his arguments, and that year I let the weeds grow freely in my orchards. It was a mistake. California is not Japan, and different conditions call for different techniques. As the dry season approached, the weeds sucked from the soil moisture that was meant for the trees, and they obstructed the operation of sprinklers. And worse, they hid a population explosion of gophers that soon were biting the roots off the trees and gnawing the bark.

So I went back to my old practice of managing the orchard floor by mowing a few times a season. I have a seven-foot flail mower with the hitch offset so that it sticks way out the right-hand side of the tractor, and I can mow nearly to the trunk without running over the tree. If we get a dry spell in January, I try to sneak in a mowing at that time. The earliest weeds to come up—mustards and radishes and fiddleneck—are speedy growers. A January mowing knocks back the early weeds, and lets the intended understory of clovers and subclovers, which start slowly, get some light and make good growth.

I mow a couple more times through the spring. If we have a lot of rain and the ground stays too wet to support a tractor, the weeds might grow tall, sometimes as much as six feet. Mowing tall weeds always draws a crowd. Tree swallows and barn swallows follow my tractor from the barn out to the orchards. As I mow, clouds of insects fly up, and the swallows zoom and dive around the tractor, scooping them up. Hawks are attracted as well; they hang overhead, keeping an eye out for little rodents that hop frantically away from the approaching tractor. I make my last mowing for the year in June; by then the weather is hot, and the ground is dry, and the weeds do not recover.

I mow only north and south, leaving in each row an unmowed strip with the tree trunks up the center of it. This is a place for beneficial insects to persist, and various other little creatures, most of whom I have no quarrels with. Sometimes, late in the summer or in the fall, I clear the unmowed strip around the trees with a scythe, to facilitate harvest.

There's a plum orchard near me that's managed according to a different philosophy. It's run by a corporate farm, and their theory is "Kill everything except the crop." They spray herbicides often—preemergent and post-emergent. They spray the trees with fungicides and insecticides—sometimes from airplanes, sometimes from the ground. They lay on so many chemicals that there is not a living thing to be found in that orchard but the plum trees—not an earthworm, not a blade of grass. The orchard has a disturbingly surrealistic aspect to it—the very regular rows of trees, and the bare earth, and the sky. The trees bear abundant fruit, and yet I'm certain that this kind of farming destroys the land. A practice with so much death connected to it cannot be right.

In dealing with nature, to be authoritarian is almost always a mistake. In the long run, things work out better if the farmer learns to tolerate complexity and ambiguity. The good farmer tries to find a point halfway in between being an obsessive neatnik and being a slob. Having found that point, it takes a good deal of attention to stay there and not slide off in one direction or the other; it's like keeping a perpetual three days' growth of beard. Having the right tools helps. Certainly, a mower is a better choice than a sprayer.

Kevin Rafferty

KEVIN RAFFERTY WAS BAFFLED BY ABSTRACT THOUGHT. If conversation departed from the concrete and literal, he immediately became confused. This made him a natural candidate for joining a fundamentalist sect, where someone else would do his thinking for him. He might have become a hard-shell Baptist, or a fundamentalist Muslim, or a Scientologist, but by chance he became an organic farmer. For Kevin, the organic movement supplied both cosmography and a guide to daily life; the organic code was his scripture and the organic inspectors were his clergy. Kevin took great comfort in belonging to the chosen minority following the one true and narrow path of organic farming—the few but righteous "us" pitted against the numerous and misguided "them." The organic religion improved on Christianity in that one did not have to wait until death for judgment; judgment came once a year with the annual organic inspection. On the other hand, the organic sect had a serious shortcoming: it lacked a charismatic founder, or a leader, or even a single name that anyone had heard much of. But the movement was young, and that might yet come to pass.

Kevin used the O-word with as much syntactic creativity as a hostile teenager uses the F-word; it was verb, noun, adverb, adjective, and interjection. It wouldn't surprise me at all if he signed his letters "Organically yours." He spoke loudly at the market, flinging out a kind of verbal salad in which the word "organic" was the principal ingredient. It was wearying to listen to him.

One week I noticed he had a new word: "holistic." I doubt if he knew precisely what it meant, but he could tell from the reaction of his customers that it carried a powerful mojo. So Kevin worked it hard, and managed to get "holistic" or "holistically" into every sentence at least once, mixing it up with "organic" and "natural" in a kind of three-part invention.

As sometimes happens in the market, just by chance, there came a time when for a few minutes there were hardly any customers, and the farmers could take a breather. I said, "Kevin, isn't it true that in organic farming the universe is divided into two halves, called the natural and the synthetic? One's good and one's bad, I forget which is which."

"Synthetic is the bad one," he said, looking at me suspiciously.

"Yes, of course," I said. "Anyway, when you split the world into two separate halves, that's not holistic, it's dualistic. Dual, as in two. Organic is not holistic, it's dualistic."

"No, you're wrong," he said. "Organic is holistic."

I thought for a moment. "Have you ever heard of pyrethrin?" I asked.

"Yeah. It's a ground-up plant, from Africa. We use it to control whiteflies on eggplant."

"Right," I said. "So here's pyrethrin, and it's an organic pesticide made from a daisy. Now, there's also synthetic pyrethrin that's made by a chemical company in New Jersey, starting from oil and carrying out chemical reactions on it. What they end up with is exactly the same as the natural pyrethrin. If you had two bottles of pyrethrin, one natural and one synthetic, they would be absolutely identical. There is no chemical test you could think of that would distinguish one from the other. And now if the labels fell off those two bottles, so you couldn't tell which was organic and which was synthetic, would it matter which bottle you put the label back on?"

"Of course it would matter," said Kevin. "The organic one is holistic and natural, the synthetic one is bad."

"But they're the same," I said. "It is a very odd notion of nature that would say one bottle is natural and one isn't."

"Why do you try to make things so confusing?"

"I was just trying to show the difference between dualistic and holistic," I said. "You're telling everyone that organic is holistic, but it's not."

"I don't agree," said Kevin. "Organic is holistic. I read it in a magazine." He turned his back to me.

Of course, it's extremely bad manners to tease someone about his religion, and Kevin is such an easy target that there's not much sport in baiting him. I don't do it out of malice, however. I am an organic farmer myself; my orchard lands are registered organic, and the apricots and citrus and quince and olives I grow are certified organic. I find this to be slightly shameful, for it implies adherence to a profoundly illogical (and dualistic) corpus of laws. A thoughtful person could no more be proud of being an organic farmer than he could be proud of being a Democrat or a Republican. The philosophical basis of the organic code is so shaky that even a drunken undergraduate eking out a C-minus grade in philosophy would have no trouble demolishing it in an argument.

In the 1960s I marched with a group of protestors against the war in Vietnam. I found myself in the midst of a large crowd who were chanting in unison, and somewhat out of tune: "All we are saying is give peace a chance." It made me very uncomfortable. I wanted to shout, "Wait a minute! Stop! That's not all I'm saying at all. I have a much more complex and specific message than that." But a mob is notoriously inarticulate. I feel the same way about "organic" as I did about "Give peace a chance." One word doesn't begin to convey the complexities of farming well or farming badly.

Fifty-something

Acording to the census for the year 2000, the median age of the residents of my market town is 25.3 years. The crowd at the market bears up the statistic; there are lots of young parents, and children, and babies, and the students seem younger every year. Even so, there are a few shoppers my age—fifty-something. And although we may be unacquainted, we acknowledge one another with a barely perceptible nod. We share a certain unspoken camaraderie, as if we were members of a slightly disreputable minority, or fellow veterans of a failed campaign.

The young people accept the world as they find it. That there is an old grizzle-chops at the market selling peonies for a dollar a stem every Wednesday in May they take for granted. This is how the world is, and why should it be otherwise? But the older shoppers realize how fragile institutions are, and individuals, and they recognize that there is no inevitability to my bringing peonies to the market, and so they thank me for bringing them.

When I was a little child, I considered grown-ups to be powerful and scary. As I became an adult myself, I saw them differently. They seemed like tasteless relics, cluttering up the landscape, and driving too slowly, and shopping indecisively, and taking the good jobs, which they did poorly. Their clothing was pathetically unfashionable, and so were their jokes and their music. It was obvious that the world belonged to us, the young. Surely we were the first generation to have discovered love, and its luscious consummations. It seemed implausible that our parents' generation had managed to procreate at all; it must have been some kind of clumsy accident. Why didn't these old fogies just get out of the way? I see that attitude now in the marketplace, chiefly among young males. They smirk when they talk to the old farmers, as if we were innately comic.

I wonder about the way in which the fifty-somethings at the market subtly acknowledge one another. I think that the roots of an answer can be found in our childhoods. In elementary school, when the weather was rainy, we had to stay in the classroom over recess and lunch period, and sometimes the teacher organized games to keep us from becoming too wild. One of her favorite games was called musical chairs. (The name makes no sense; it must be a corruption of "music and chairs.") Chairs were set in a circle, facing outward, their number being one less than the number of children. The children paraded around the chairs while music played on an old record player. When the teacher unexpectedly stopped the music by lifting the needle from the record, we each had to claim a chair and sit in it. Amid an outburst of squealing and shoving, we each got a place—all but one of us. The chairless one, forlornly standing while the others sat, was cast out of the game, together with another chair. The game continued until there were just one chair and two children left, and finally, just the winner.

I found the game of musical chairs to be anxiety-provoking, and it was with mixed disappointment and relief that I was booted out when I couldn't find a chair. The message of the game was clear enough: there are not enough goods to go around, and so you must elbow your comrades out of the way in order to claim your share. Slightly more than your share, actually. The game trained children for survival by aggression in a culture of scarcity. I expect that it was popular during the Great Depression, which was when my teacher learned it. But it was the wrong game for us. We were to grow up in a world of abundance, not scarcity. We needed a different set of values and techniques, and they weren't given to us. Some learned the lesson of musical chairs too well, and went on to amass piles of needless wealth, crushing any who got in their way. Others figured out on their own a gentler way of living.

By now, most of the fifty-somethings have come to terms with the material world. Most of us accept our place in society. And most of us have unlearned the inappropriate lesson of musical chairs. So many of our comrades have stumbled and fallen and wound up in the obituaries that if now we were to play the game, there would be an excess of chairs. We could be solicitous of one another. "Here, let me help you find a comfortable chair," we would say. "I hope that troublesome knee isn't bothering you much today." There would be no need at all for an elbow in the ribs. There never was. Perhaps, in that slight greeting with which we acknowledge one another, we commiserate about the false path along which we were guided, and we apologize for our slowness in recognizing our error.

Foraging

THERE IS A SCRAP OF ABANDONED ALMOND ORCHARD half a mile to the west of us, and we have permission of the owner to gather nuts. Late in September I set out with my two daughters, dragging a wagon and a couple of buckets. The earliest almond to ripen is a variety called Nonpareil. The nuts are aristocratic—slender and elongated—the shells thin and papery. You can twist the shell off with your fingers. Nonpareil is most highly thought of in commerce and fetches the highest price. But as with other tree crops, the farmer needs several varieties mixed together in his orchard to get good pollination and fruit set, so every third row in the orchard is another variety—Carmel or Mission or Ne Plus Ultra. The late varieties are of a peasant build—compact and stocky, with tough shells and good flavor. I prefer them. And anyway, the crows and squirrels take all the Nonpareils, which are easily shelled out, so by the time we go nut gathering, Missions are all that are left.

I first took my younger daughter on one of these expeditions when she was fifteen months old. Her ability to gather nuts was surprising. With those chubby fingers she could pluck up the nuts and plonk them into a bucket nearly as fast as I could. It occurred to me that this knack must be deeply embedded in our genes, similar to the way a fledgling finch can unerringly peck up a tiny seed from among grains of sand without having been taught how. An ability to forage seems a part of our primate heritage, too firmly anchored in our biology to be swept away by mere civilization.

When I was ten years old, I had a well-developed route of seasonal foraging. I knew places on the rough edges of almond orchards where I could pick up nuts. I knew where the branches of a cherry tree hung over a fence into an alley, and where a fig tree persisted at a burned-out homestead. There was a place along the Southern Pacific railroad tracks where a bridge spanned a little slough; sweet blackberries grew there. There were certain trees with especially good walnuts, and there was a row of unguarded kumquats that provided fruit into January. A pineapple guava bush grew under a water tower; it was surrounded by chain-link fence, but I could poke a stick through the wires and roll the fallen fruits to a little hollow, where I could pull them under the fence. A tangerine tree by the library was easily climbed, and no one seemed to mind. I knew a place at the College of Agriculture where there was a loquat tree, where one could snitch the first spring fruits long before cherries were ready. In summer, tomatoes could always be found, these being the principal crop of the region, but there were also peach trees around town, and an unvalued apricot tree by a barn. It seems that every fence had a grapevine on it—they were hardly ever far from reach. There was a sassafras tree by the high school from which one could worry off a bit of root to chew on. The seeds of wild fennel also were good for chewing on, and had the taste of licorice. Canary Island date palms grew by the train station; the dates were almost entirely seed, but the thin coating of flesh was pure sugar. Certain pomegranate bushes rather too near the sidewalk seemed to need some of their heavy fruits harvested to avoid bonking passersby. A pal and I spent hours combing through a patch of oxalis that grew on the shady side of an abutment, seeking the little pods with their sharp, sour taste.

Although I had the abundant harvest of conventional agriculture set before me at the table every evening, at that stage of my life I enjoyed at the same time an aboriginal economy of hunting and gathering. My friends and I did not see anything exceptional in this; it was an unexamined fact of life that we knew what could be freely eaten and where it could be found. Aside from the pineapple guava bush, which had been pointed out to me by my father, the forages were discovered by simply roaming about with open eyes and a receptive mind—and by daring each other to taste fruits that looked like they might be poisonous.

I didn't spend as many hours roaming as I wished: during many of the daylight hours I squirmed in a chair in school while the teachers tried to civilize us. Hours of boredom and confinement in the classroom were training for a life of office work. As the years went by, most of us capitulated, for our culture punishes those who do not. We forgot about foraging, and learned to buy our food at the supermarket, and became useful cogs in society's machinery. But it is reassuring to know that when the fragile vessel of civilization founders, which surely it will, the survivors will have at the ready innate foraging skills—suppressed perhaps, but hardly diminished—to buoy them along. Ten-year-old boys ought to adapt easily.

Which brings me back around to the subject of wild almonds. One June evening we met at Chez Panisse for a dinner in honor of my sister's birthday. (It is the only time I have eaten there—penniless farmers don't frequent such spots.) We were served a soup made from unripe almonds—a mixture of bitter wild ones as well as sweet ones. In June, two months before the nuts are ripe, the almonds are full size but have not yet hardened, and they have the texture of thick cream. It seems exotic, if not far-fetched, to make soup from such an ingredient, but it is not difficult to imagine a bad year in Spain—late storms, failed crops, war, chaos—and a desperately hungry peasant gathering unripe bitter almonds from a wild tree in a ravine so as to have something to put in his growling stomach. And with refinements, this soup evolved into an elegant and subtle dish. We take what we have, and make a virtue of it.

Persimmons

THE WORDS TO AN OLD TUNE GO "Possum in the 'simmon tree /
Raccoon on the ground / Raccoon says, 'Mr. Possum / Won't you
shake them 'simmons down?'" To judge by the gnawed fruit littering
the ground and the broken branches in the tree, both Mr. Possum
and Mr. Raccoon have been up the 'simmon tree lately, along with
their cousins and their aunts. It is an odd thing in this fertile valley
that there is hardly any fruit to be had in the fall. Such apples as
grow here—Fuji and Gala and Braeburn—are harvested in
September, and until the tangerines come in at Christmastime, persimmons are about the only game in town. Possum and raccoon
know this; so do blue jay and mockingbird, and field mouse and
ground squirrel.

We grow two kinds of persimmons: Fuyus and Hachiyas. The
Fuyu has a flattened fruit, like a good-sized tomato, and you can eat
it at an early stage when it has turned orange but is still crunchy. We
send our daughter to school with a Fuyu persimmon in her pocket
the way a New Englander would send his child with an apple.

The Hachiya has a pointed fruit, and when unripe it is highly
astringent. If you bite into an unripe Hachiya, it will suck all the
moisture out of the lining of your mouth, and leave you with a pucker
for half a day. Even the birds leave unripe Hachiyas alone. The
astringency disappears only when the fruit is dead ripe and the flesh
has turned to liquid. This is a mess to eat out of hand—a leathery
skin full of liquid—but the pulp can be gotten into a bowl and then

used in every sort of baking—muffins, breads, pancakes, cookies, puddings, even the morning bowl of oatmeal. We also pick unripe Hachiyas and peel them and hang them up to dry in the rafters of the barn; they slowly wither and shrink, and sugar crystallizes on the surface, and they achieve the consistency and sweetness of a Medjool date.

The persimmon tree has long, soft, fuzzy leaves, like donkey's ears, that attest to its tropical origins. After the first frost, the leaves are shed and the brilliant orange fruits remain on the otherwise barren tree. If you rub the waxy bloom from a persimmon, the skin shines beautifully; it is even more orange than an orange. When you have trouble in an apple tree, it shows up as the color red—a red leaf, a premature red spot on a fruit. In the persimmon, trouble is black. There is a streak of blackness that runs through the tribe, showing up in fruit and bark and leaf, and the black cabinet wood ebony comes from an African persimmon. As the season progresses, the orange fruits may become burnished with black, or they may show black halos around bird pecks.

In 1929, at a time when most tractors were gray, the Allis-Chalmers Tractor Company astounded the farming world by painting its new tractors persimmon orange. The orange tractors were a great success, perhaps because they hinted that there might be more to farming than drudgery, and perhaps because, like the fruit they imitated, they carried a cheerful note through a tough season. I used to have a 1948 Allis-Chalmers tractor, and one drab November day, being in a whimsical mood, I parked it under a persimmon tree just to see the composition. The tractor's paint was faded, but the persimmons shone like lanterns.

Old Basque

ONE WEDNESDAY EVENING, during a slow market, I leaned against my truck and watched the shoppers—families, couples, students, eccentrics. I noticed an old man with close-cropped gray hair wandering among the stands. I would guess from his face that he was past seventy years old; yet he was still agile. He wore old-fashioned trousers with a length of cotton rope in place of a belt, and his white shirt was frayed at the cuffs and collar, but clean. Something about his dress, or the shape of his head, or the way he moved led me to think that he was a Basque.

Basques came to our district to herd sheep, which they still do. They also do all the sheep shearing hereabouts. One of my neighbors keeps sheep, and one day I happened along when shearing was in progress. The shearer had attached a rope to a bolt in the ceiling of the shearing shed. The other end of the rope held a wide leather harness that went around his waist, so that he could float horizontally a few feet above the floor like a dragonfly, or an angel. The shed was only about eight feet square, and he maneuvered by kicking off the walls. A sheep would come in; he would float over it, his shears clicking away, and after two or two and a half minutes he'd slap the now naked sheep on the rump to send it out the exit, and the perfect fleece would be laid on top of a pile. It was a wonderful performance—a sort of rustic ballet. If he had been plying his art in a theater, the audience would have leapt to their feet and cheered.

The old Basque man in the market came up to my stand, where I was selling melons. He studied them carefully, turning them a little this way or that, and after a while found the one he was looking for, a small melon of a variety called Rayyan that is superficially like a cantaloupe but juicier, and sweeter, and more fragrant. The little polygons defined by the netting on its skin were orange grading into gold, like a gaudy sunset. I continued leaning against my truck, waiting for the moment when I might be needed. He examined the melon from every angle. He held it to his face and closed his eyes and inhaled its fragrance. He held it at arm's length and stroked it gently with his fingertips, as if it were the cheek of his lover. After a while he looked to me and said, "Tell me about this melon." I explained about the variety, and where I grew them, and how to judge ripeness. He was full of questions, and I explained to him my system of planting oats in the fall into ground harrowed perfectly flat, and then mowing the oats the following spring to leave a thick layer of oat hay on the ground, and then transplanting melon seedlings into the mulch of hay without any tillage.

"How much is it?" he asked.

These melons usually run about five to six pounds, and I had been selling them for fifty cents a pound, but to him I said, "One dollar." He nodded, and slowly pulled a dollar from his pocket and handed it to me.

"You know," he said, "on Saturday I bought two apples, and they are so beautiful that I cannot bring myself to eat them." He sighed and looked at his melon. Probably it, too, was too beautiful to eat. He walked off through the market, cradling his melon like a cherished grandchild.

A melon is a marvelous and astonishing thing—surely the world without melons would be a poorer place—and every melon deserves that kind of affectionate attention, as does every other piece of fruit, and head of cabbage, and handful of beans. Our culture is so impoverished in wonderment that one seeking a thrill thinks of skiing down a vertical slope, or jumping out of an airplane, but if he only had the wits and the spirit, he could experience a deeper thrill by lying in a meadow and watching a beetle climb a stalk of grass, or by admiring a melon.

It occurred to me that the Basque's sensitivity might have been sharpened by some recent close meeting with death. You're lying there at the side of the road, your heart thumping, the pain almost unbearable, waiting for the ambulance, and you turn your head to the side, and you see a humble clump of little weeds and grasses against a rock. You think, "My god, how beautiful they are, how exquisite in every detail, I could watch them for hours, days even. How is it that I have been rushing through life so fast that I have not seen them until now?" It is in such an extreme circumstance that an apple becomes too beautiful to eat.

A little later in the market, my friend Danielle came by. She's an artist and a feminist and an activist, and she told me about an exhibit she was organizing of posters of environmental art. She ranted for a while against useless art, and pretty art, and especially against the art departments of universities. I heard her out, but I didn't entirely agree with her. When I was about thirteen years old, I was one day leafing through some art books in the library (probably, at that age, looking for nudes), and I came across a fifteenth-century painting by Albrecht Dürer of a humble clump of little weeds and grasses against a rock. They were drawn with such care, and so lovingly, that I felt as if I were seeing the plants for the first time. The page entranced me. I got no further in the book. Danielle might call it useless art, or pretty art, but it taught me something important about how to see, as it must have taught countless others.

Thinking about Dürer's weeds led my mind back to the Basque. Perhaps he hadn't had a brush with death after all. Perhaps he was a relict fifteenth-century man, a contemporary of Dürer, a shepherd who lived far back in the hills following a simple life with his flock, untroubled by any electronic image, or any written word, or even much of any spoken word. Such a one could pass a day admiring a clump of weeds and grasses against a mossy rock and think it a day well used. Such a one, too, would have the leisure, and the innocence, and the imagination, to fall in love with a melon.

We believe that we are well off, only because we no longer know what it is that we have lost.

Mowing with a Scythe

I BOUGHT MY SCYTHE IN A SECONDHAND BOOKSTORE that occupied a series of rooms in the basement of an old building. Overhead one could see the stout joists of the floor above. In one of the back rooms I happened to glance up, and noticed a scythe hanging on two wooden pegs let into a joist. The scythe was extraordinarily beautiful, with a complex, three-dimensional shape to its handle and a long, curved steel blade. It was just like the one that the grim reaper carries. A clerk was shelving books nearby. I said, "Excuse me, is that scythe for sale?"

"You'd have to ask the owner. He's out front."

At the front of the store, an old man with half-glasses was hunched over the counter, chin in hand, reading. "I was wondering if the scythe hanging from the ceiling in the back room is for sale," I said.

"Scythe?" he said. "Hanging from the ceiling? You'd better show me."

We walked to the back room and I pointed it out. The owner stared at it. "I've been in this store twenty-two years, and I never saw that before."

"Would you consider selling it?" I asked.

"I don't see why not," he said.

I had to borrow a stepladder from a place up the street to reach the scythe. The clerk and I wrapped the sharp blade in a sheath of newspaper tied with cotton string so that I was able to navigate the crowded sidewalks back to my truck without inadvertently harvesting any souls.

I bought the scythe not with the intention of putting it to work, but simply because it was beautiful. I hung it on a peg on the wall of my toolshed, where I could admire it several times a day. The wooden handle (called a snath) is a tapered cylinder of ash, twisted into a gentle spiral. Attached to it are two wooden pegs (the nibs) that are grasped by the reaper. They are fastened to the snath by a metal connector that has a left-handed thread, so that in use the nibs tighten themselves instead of becoming loose.

Scythes show up in the sixteenth-century paintings and engravings of Pieter Brueghel, but those scythes have straight snaths. The curved snath evolved incrementally and anonymously during the eighteenth and nineteenth centuries. It is perfectly designed to fit the human body at work. The reaper grasps the nibs and executes a comfortable, rhythmic, swaying motion, almost a dance. This propels the metal blade along an arc parallel to the ground, and at an angle so that it slices rather than chops the stalks of grain. (As a child I read in a book some advice that has stuck with me; it was from a Turkish cavalry officer instructing a novice about lopping off heads in battle: "Don't chop. Slice.")

In addition to two ancient scythes (the second was given to me), I also have some sickles. The sickle is a small cousin of the scythe, a curved blade with a short handle, meant for one-handed work. I bought the first sickle at a junk shop with the intention of using it to clear weeds in tight quarters, a job it did well. Then I found another. At that point it became a collection, and now I have half a dozen, all slightly different, hanging on the wall of the toolshed.

The neural architecture of the human brain is especially wired for appreciating arrays of objects that are similar but not quite the same. We find a museum case of related beetles, or an album of family photographs, to be endlessly interesting as we sort out individuality and familiality. We are predisposed to become taxonomists. My little display of sickles is a wordless essay in taxonomy.

One of the sickles has a very deep curve, like the sickle on the old Soviet flag. The Soviet Union was a repressive and despotic government, hardly to be admired, but I find their choice of national symbols (hammer and sickle—industry and agriculture) to be far more appealing than the idle and rapacious eagle of the Americans.

Anyway, I bought the sickles for the purpose of using them, and found them to be fast and effective tools. And it was because of success with the sickles that it occurred to me to take my scythe down from its peg and try it at its intended purpose. My first attempt was a failure, for it was early spring, and I was scything lush, wet weeds. The work was exhausting, and in five minutes I was whipped. The scythe properly comes into use later in the season, when weeds have dried out and their stems have stiffened. Scything dried weeds late in summer is pleasant, soothing, aerobic exercise, like waltzing. And progress is rapid. In places where a tractor doesn't fit, I can go in with a scythe and clear ground quickly and effectively. For me, the scythe is no longer just a shapely and interesting device; it has become one of the tools that I regularly depend on.

Traditionally, a scythe was sharpened not with a stone, but with a little hammer. A whetstone grinds the metal edge into a fine dust while it sharpens, so that in the course of a few seasons the blade is worn away and requires replacement. To many a reaper, this would be an intolerable expense. Instead, when the blade was dull, he would tap it with a hammer, gradually flattening the leading edge until it was once again sharp, without having ground off any metal. I've tried it both ways. In my hands the stone does a better job, but nonetheless I occasionally sharpen the blade with a little hammer just for the pleasure of the experience. Tap-tap, tap-tap, tap-tap.

If you wanted to buy a scythe today, you could go to your local old-fashioned hardware store—potbellied guys with suspenders adding up the sums with a pencil on the back of a paper bag. Or you could go to a modern chain store—a fifty-acre concrete box full of goods from China. Neither one would have a scythe. They're not available anymore. Instead, they would try to sell you a string trimmer—a nasty little two-stroke motor on a metal stick that causes a plastic string to whirl around. The operator stands in the midst of ear-wracking noise, breathing the fumes of burnt oil and shredding the weeds with the string, as often as not flaying the bark from a tree while he's at it. The string trimmer's only virtue, if it is a virtue, is that neither skill nor strength is required to use it.

This is another case of something subtle and old and excellent being replaced by something obnoxious and violent and inferior. Call it progress, and apply enough advertising to it, and people will fall for it. Not all of them, however.

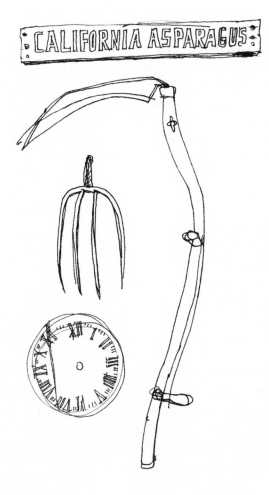

Beyond Farming

I ATTENDED MY COLLEGE GRADUATION, but I did not wear a cap and gown, and I did not sit with my classmates. I wore old blue jeans and a work shirt, and I crept under a bush and lay on the ground to listen to the speeches. My diploma arrived in the mail three weeks later.

At college I didn't feel the sense of entitlement, or the sense of belonging, shared by my classmates, most of them the offspring of wealthy and powerful families. I sat in the back row of the lecture hall, and it was as if the professor were lecturing to the authentic students in front of me, and I was merely eavesdropping. At any moment I half expected to be asked to leave.

An academic scholarship covered the cost of tuition, but I still had to work twenty or thirty hours a week to meet my other expenses. And so while my classmates were wielding a tennis racket or a martini glass or a slender volume of verse, I was wielding a broom or a rake or a paintbrush. I had one foot in the world of labor and the other foot in a famous university, and in both places I was an imposter.

At the time of my graduation I was working on the small crew that would set up thirteen thousand folding chairs for the graduation ceremony. We finished the last row just as the academic procession entered the quad. That's when I crept under my bush to hear the speeches. Two hours later, we would start folding up the thirteen thousand chairs and stacking them on dollies so they could be hauled to the next event.

A shrewd old professor gave a speech. He warned the graduates that in their chosen careers, after ten or a dozen years, they would likely be overcome with doubt as to whether they had made the right choice. In the early years they would be preoccupied with passing exams and getting licensed and joining their professions: engaging in their first surgeries, or lectures, or lawsuits, or audits, or whatever their profession entailed. These would be heady times. But then would come a stage when novelty gave way to routine, and that was the dangerous time. The excitement would have gone out of the job. Decades of uneventful repetition would stretch out ahead. One might be tempted to switch to a different career. The speaker warned against this. He said that after a couple of years of burnout, one's interest would rekindle, and then one could continue as a master craftsman in his chosen field. The thrill of novelty would have passed, but there would be a mature satisfaction in skillfully performing one's profession.

I believe the old codger was at least half right. Almost everyone I know reached that stage in their careers when the novelty had passed, and they realized that they were faced with another twenty-five years of routine before they retired. Most were starting families at this time and couldn't easily change careers, so they stuck with their choice and made the best of it. It wasn't so bad. But some of us realized we had made errors and, summoning up our courage, started over in a new field. Farming was my fourth career, after three false starts in other directions. I was deficient in self-knowledge, and it took that long for me to find my destiny.

On the subject of destiny I'm ambivalent. On the one hand, we have only one life, and it would be tragic to waste it in an unsatisfactory profession simply because one lacked the gumption to find one's true place. On the other hand, to be given meaningful work is a privilege and a blessing; it is best to accept one's fate graciously, and not be so self-indulgent about seeking one's destiny. (The same remarks might be applied to finding a spouse as finding a career; some are happy to accept an adequate match, others feel propelled to seek out their destiny, whatever the cost.)

As I mentioned, I had three careers before becoming a farmer. In retrospect, I'm grateful that I was able to admit my mistakes and start over again at the beginning until I found a truly suitable profession. Farming is what I have done the longest and been happiest at. But I am not convinced that I will keep at farming forever. I think I might have one more career left in me. I imagine it like this.

I would live in an isolated coastal town somewhere in the farther end of the Southern Hemisphere, perhaps in Chile. It should be a place only one notch above poverty, so that everyone has wholesome food to eat, and a soft place to sleep, but not much beyond that. Wealth is the enemy of tranquility, and of justice, and of conservation; best not to have too much of it around. I would set myself up as the village baker. Each morning I would arise at three a.m. and bicycle through the dark and quiet streets to my bakery. There I would light my ovens, and fetch a sack of flour from the storeroom, and pop a disk into the CD player: Bach, or Boccherini, or Monteverdi. Later, while the bread was baking, I would stand in the open doorway, watching the dawn construct itself and listening to the town come to life.

I would bake just four kinds of bread: a sourdough baguette, a *pain levain*, a whole wheat bread with raisins and nuts, and a sourdough with Kalamata olives and rosemary. Four breads; that's enough. About ten in the morning my wife would come in to bake whatever pastry might be required—maybe even a wedding cake. And then I would take baskets of bread on my bicycle and make my deliveries to the cafés and restaurants, stopping to trade jokes with the cooks and kitchen help.

In the afternoon I would work for a few hours in my garden, or practice Bach suites on the 'cello. At three o'clock I would drop in at the orphanage to tutor some of the students who were finding their studies difficult. On the way home I would go by the docks to see how the day's catch was, and to pick up a fish for dinner (company coming, better get a big one). I might stop in at the tavern for a glass of beer and a game of dominoes.

I would not listen to a radio, nor subscribe to any newspaper. By now I know well enough what passes for news—strife and stupidity and senselessness. I have heard more than enough of it for one lifetime. Of the outside world and its history I would live in undisturbed ignorance.

On Saturdays I would bake double, and take half to the farmers' market. There I could greet my friends who are farmers and trade recipes with my customers. As I passed out loaves of bread, still warm from the oven, people would tell me of the local happenings: who got married, who had a baby, who died, whose child is showing astounding skill at the violin. And in turn I would share whatever bits of news I had. Is this not how human beings were meant to live?

MIKE MADISON lives with his wife, Dianne, in Winters, California, where they operate a small truck farm in the Sacramento Valley. His previous book, *Walking the Flatlands*, is available from Heyday Books.

GREAT VALLEY

Great Valley Books is an imprint of Heyday Books, Berkeley, California. Created in 2002 with a grant from The James Irvine Foundation and with the support of the Great Valley Center (Modesto, California), it strives to promote the rich literary, artistic, and cultural resources of California's Central Valley by publishing books of the highest merit and broadest interest.

Great Valley Books and other Central Valley titles published by Heyday Books:

Walking the Flatlands: The Rural Landscape of the Lower Sacramento Valley, *by Mike Madison*

Haslam's Valley, *by Gerald Haslam*

Workin' Man Blues: Country Music in California, *by Gerald Haslam, with Alexandra Haslam Russell and Richard Chon*

Peace Is a Four-Letter Word, *by Janet Nichols Lynch*

Magpies and Mayflies: An Introduction to Plants and Animals of the Central Valley and the Sierra Foothills, *by Derek Madden, Ken Charters, and Cathy Snyder*

Lion Singer, *by Sylvia Ross*

Dream Songs and Ceremony: Reflections on Traditional California Indian Dance, *by Frank LaPena*

Two-Hearted Oak: The Photography of Roman Loranc, *with text by Lillian Vallee*

Bloodvine, *by Aris Janigian*

Structures of Utility, *by David Stark Wilson*

Highway 99: A Literary Journey through California's Great Central Valley, *edited by Stan Yogi*

How Much Earth: The Fresno Poets, *edited by Christopher Buckley, David Oliveira, and M. L. Williams*

Picturing California's Other Landscape, *edited by Heath Schenker*

Indian Summer: Traditional Life among the Choinumne Indians, *by Thomas Jefferson Mayfield*

Heyday

HEYDAY INSTITUTE

Since its founding in 1974, Heyday Books has occupied a unique niche in the publishing world, specializing in books that foster an understanding of California history, literature, art, environment, social issues, and culture. We are a 501(c)(3) nonprofit organization based in Berkeley, California, serving a wide range of people and audiences throughout California and beyond. Our commitment is to enhance California's rich cultural heritage by providing a platform for writers, poets, artists, scholars, and storytellers who help keep this diverse legacy alive.

We are grateful for the generous funding we've received for our publications and programs during the past year from foundations and more than 300 individuals. Major recent supporters include:

Anonymous; Arroyo Fund; Bay Tree Fund; California Association of Resource Conservation Districts; California Oak Foundation; Candelaria Fund; CANfit; Columbia Foundation; Colusa Indian Community Council; Flow Fund Circle; Wallace Alexander Gerbode Foundation; Richard and Rhoda Goldman Fund; Evelyn & Walter Haas, Jr. Fund; Walter & Elise Haas Fund; Hopland Band of Pomo Indians; James Irvine Foundation; Guy Lampard; Jeff Lustig; George Fredrick Jewett Foundation; LEF Foundation; David Mas Masumoto; James McClatchy; Michael McCone; Gordon and Betty Moore Foundation; Morongo Band of Mission Indians; National Endowment for the Arts; National Park Service; Ed Penhoet; Rim of the World Interpretive Association; Riverside/San Bernardino County Indian Health; River Rock Casino; Alan Rosenus; John-Austin Saviano/Moore Foundation; Sandy Cold Shapero; Ernest and June Siva; LJ and Mary Skaggs Foundation; Strong Foundation for Environmental Values; Swinerton Family Fund; and the Harold and Alma White Memorial Fund.

For more information about Heyday Institute, our publications and programs, please visit our website at www.heydaybooks.com.